Doris Stokes, the celebrated clairaudient, passed over on 8 May 1987. Throughout her years as a medium she confounded sceptics with the uncanny accuracy of her readings and become internationally famous due to her numerous sell-out demonstrations and her many television and radio appearances both here and abroad.

Linda Dearsley knew Doris Stokes for nearly ten years and worked with her on six of her seven volumes of autobiography. An author of a number of books, Linda Dearsley is also a freelance journalist working on national magazines and newspapers.

The seven volumes of Doris Stokes'
autobiography

Written with Linda Dearsley:

VOICES IN MY EAR: THE AUTOBIOGRAPHY OF A MEDIUM
MORE VOICES IN MY EAR
INNOCENT VOICES IN MY EAR
WHISPERING VOICES
VOICES OF LOVE
JOYFUL VOICES

Written with Pam and Mike Kiddey:

A HOST OF VOICES

A Tribute to Doris Stokes

Compiled by Linda Dearsley

A Futura Book

First published in Great Britain in 1988
by Futura Publications, a Division of
Macdonald & Co (Publishers) Ltd
London & Sydney

ISBN 0 7088 3679 8

Typeset, printed and bound in Great Britain by
Hazwll Watson & Viney Limited
Member of BPCC plc
Aylesbury, Bucks, England

Futura Publications
A Division of
Macdonald & Co (Publishers) Ltd
Greater London House
Hampstead Road
London NW1 7QX

A member of Maxwell Pergamon Publishing Corporation plc

Acknowledgements

The author and publisher would like to thank all those who have contributed to this book, and especially Laurie O'Leary who gave so much of his time in helping to compile this tribute to Doris Stokes.
Our apologies to all those whose tributes arrived too late for publication.

Introduction

It was lunchtime on a cool, grey day in early spring. Doris Stokes was sitting in her favourite chair looking out over the tiny garden and crumbling her sandwich into minute pieces on her plate.

She was a large woman, long resigned to wearing 'rent a tent' dresses, as she called them, on stage, yet she ate very little. This was one more meal that would end up on the bird-table.

We were working on Doris' forthcoming book, *Joyful Voices*, and as usual Doris was thinking aloud into a tape-recorder. Some people can do this, some people can't. Doris was very good at it and if she sometimes strayed from the point it didn't matter, we could sort it out later.

Before we'd started eating, Doris had been talking about her father. He was a remarkable man by all accounts, uneducated but wise, and though he died when she was only thirteen he remained a powerful influence in her life.

But suddenly, for no apparent reason, Doris changed the subject.

'You know, I was thinking about epitaphs the other day,' she said.

I must have looked surprised.

'I don't know why. I think I'd been watching something on television,' she went on. 'But d'you know, I heard this spirit voice say: "Your time on earth is over, your life in spirit is begun, when you stand before the master we know he'll say well done . . ." Isn't that beautiful?'

The sandwich turned to rubber in my mouth. I was used to Doris' spirit rhymes. At difficult moments in her life, she told me, her guide often gave her words of comfort in the form of easily-remembered pieces of verse. These simple poems weren't Shakespeare but they helped, and many of her readers with whom she shared them found them just as comforting as Doris did.

But this was different. This little rhyme had a peculiarly personal tone to it – almost as if Doris was being told that her time was up.

Yet Doris seemed quite unconscious of this interpretation.

'Isn't that lovely?' she repeated. 'Wouldn't it be wonderful to feel you'd earned an epitaph like that?'

I mumbled something non-commital through a mouthful of bread and glanced more closely at Doris. She looked well enough – or at least as well as she ever did. In recent years her health had been poor. She was one of those people who seemed to catch every virus going and she staggered from one course of antibiotics to another, always apparently just getting over something or just going down with something.

She had had her share of 'bugs' that winter. More worryingly, she had also suffered a fainting fit just before Christmas and, for all her fragile health, she wasn't the fainting type. The doctor ordered her to hospital for tests but Doris came out after a few days, apparently restored to health, having been diagnosed as suffering from nothing more 'serious' than pleurisy and exhaustion.

Some people might have been alarmed at this news – for Doris it was a relief. After several cancer operations over the years, pleurisy and exhaustion seemed trivial matters hardly worth mentioning.

She returned home to throw herself into the Christmas preparations and in the New Year she crossed London on a bitterly cold day when the snow lay on even the busiest city streets, to visit a friend and her newborn baby.

Now it was spring and, while not exactly blooming with vitality, Doris seemed reasonably well.

'All I need is a bit of sunshine and a few days down at the cottage,' she'd say whenever anyone suggested she should rest. And she was probably right.

And yet that rhyme . . . Doris was seldom wrong when she made a prediction even though she insisted she was no fortune-teller.

Doris, however, seemed quite unperturbed. She repeated the words into the tape-recorder in the hope that other people would be inspired, as she was, to earn such an epitaph.

Spring advanced, the daffodils and hyacinths in Doris' garden burst into flower and everything seemed normal.

Occasionally she complained of a headache or earache and she suffered her usual colds and bugs but nothing too alarming. Then one evening waiting to go on stage at a theatre demonstration, Doris was suddenly overcome by dizziness.

'I went hot and cold, everything swung round,' she said afterwards. 'I don't know how I got through that night. Yet funnily enough everyone said how good it was.'

Once again though, Doris seemed recovered and apparently none the worse for her peculiar 'turn'. But the same thing happened on several more occasions. Doris was particularly disappointed when a dizzy spell forced her to leave her first and last Royal Film Premiere before the film had even started. She had been looking forward to the event so much and treated herself to a special dress. Her hair, make-up and nails were perfect and she was thrilled at the prospect of mixing with the celebrities.

Yet it was all for nothing. She left after only a few minutes in her plush seat, too ill to enjoy the evening.

It was all so strange that she began to wonder if the cause could be psychological. Despite her calm exterior, Doris was highly-strung and she got very nervous before a show. She was always conscious of the fact that she had no script or act. She relied totally on her 'voices' and she worried that one night they might let her down.

She recorded many of her demonstrations to aid her memory when she was recalling events for her books, and listening to the tapes it was obvious that some nights the voices were slower to arrive than others.

I don't think she ever committed her opening words to paper but Doris' introductory chat with the audience was always more or less the same. Such an opening was necessary, she felt, because many of the people in the theatre had never seen a medium before and were nervous. They needed reassuring that nothing spooky or frightening was going to take place.

The chat was necessary for another reason too. Doris explained that she needed time to adjust to the audience and time to allow the voices to come through. Sometimes they were there almost at once, she said, in which case, after a brief line or two and a couple of jokes she would launch straight into the demonstration. But on other occasions the voices were muffled and indistinct, too vague, she said, for a confident start. When that happened she talked on, telling the audience about her home or her dog or some little family anecdote – anything to fill the gap.

Occasionally the introduction would extend to almost twice its usual length and I'd begin to fear that she would never get started at all. Then, without warning, Doris would break off almost mid-sentence and she was away, messages flying in all directions.

The audience never seemed to notice any delay and Doris showed no signs of panic, but nevertheless as the minutes ticked by and nothing happened it must have been nerve-wracking. The more that was expected of her the more difficult it must have become. So if at last her nerves were cracking under the strain it was hardly surprising.

Doris even wondered if she could be suffering from a form of agoraphobia because the dizzy spells seemed to occur when she was away from home. She didn't know a lot about phobias but as a trained nurse she was well aware that mental conditions could produce very real physical symptoms.

She was still toying with this idea when another health problem cropped up. This time it was severe earache.

I arrived one morning to take notes during a sitting which was to be included in Doris' new book *Joyful Voices*. The family had lost a son in the Zeebrugge ferry disaster and they thought it would be nice if the boy could be remembered in print.

When Doris came to the door she looked dreadful. She was still in her dressing-gown, her face pale and waxy, her hands trembling.

'I tried to phone to stop you coming but you'd already left,' she said, 'and the family are on their way too. I don't know what I'm going to do. They're coming such a long way and I feel terrible. I don't think I'll be able to work.'

She had such an earache that her head felt it would split in two, she explained, and it was making her feel dizzy. The doctor suspected a sinus infection.

To make matters worse the house was in chaos. There were blocked drains outside and builders were hurrying to and fro, making phone calls and asking questions about the water supply. Doris' manager, Laurie O'Leary, had come over to try to sort out the mess and there seemed to be people everywhere.

As usual, Doris' main concern was that the bereaved family would have embarked on a wasted journey.

'They'll understand, I'm sure,' I said, helping Doris back to her chair.

She barely had time for a cup of tea and a painkiller before there was a knock at the door. The family had arrived.

Of course, Doris had intended to apologise for her ill-health and their wasted journey, but once they were actually seated on her sofa she couldn't turn them away without making an effort.

'I don't suppose this'll be any good,' she warned, 'but I'll try.'

She tried and soon the messages were pouring out. The family was delighted and but for Doris' dressing-gown and sadly wan appearance, no one would have guessed that she was unwell.

Later, when the family had gone, Doris subsided wearily into her favourite armchair. She was very tired and her head was worse than ever yet somehow she was cheerful.

'I didn't think I could do it but that wasn't too bad, was it?' she said. 'They seemed a lot happier when they left. I think I did a bit of good today.'

The next morning she felt a little better and gradually the 'sinus infection' seemed to ease. it was responding to the antibiotics, Doris felt sure.

Over the next few weeks she was not exactly well but neither did she appear too ill.

Then at Easter Doris collapsed again. She was admitted to hospital once more and this time a brain tumour was discovered.

At once, all the worrying little symptoms fell into place: the headaches, the earaches, the dizziness. Even the difficulties with her memory. When we'd started working on Doris' first book, *Voices In My Ear*, in the 1970s, Doris' memory had been excellent, but since then it had deteriorated. In the past year it had become increasingly difficult for her to remember the minute details she needed for her books and so she'd fallen into the habit of tape-recording as much of her work as possible. Without the recordings, names and important facts often eluded her.

Of course Doris was getting older and she had suffered a stroke. It was easy to find plausible ex-planations. On the other hand she was only sixty-seven – not much older than the Prime Minister, after all, and the stroke had been minor one. Now the real reason for her problems was clear. Apparently the brain tumour was quite large and she must have been suffering the effects for some time without realizing it.

In hospital Doris remained cheerful, courageous and outwardly optimistic.

'Fortunately they can operate,' she explained. 'But it'll be a few months before I can get back to work.'

She sat in bed leafing through the pages of her manuscript even though her eyesight had become too blurred to read it properly. She was anxious, too, about a forthcoming radio interview she had promised to do.

'Perhaps they could bring it forward and I could record it from the hospital,' she said. 'I've got a couple of days before the operation.'

She wouldn't hear of suggestions that perhaps she wasn't well enough.

'Of course I am. I can manage an interview as long as I don't have to go anywhere,' she insisted.

She was also worried about her hair. That springy white hair which for so long had resisted her attempts to get it fully under control would have to be shaved off before the operation.

'It'll take ages to grow again,' said Doris. 'I'll have to wear a turban.'

And Laurie was despatched to find a selection of pretty turbans so that Doris wouldn't frighten her visitors with the sight of a shaved head.

Yes, she was optimistic, yet she was also thinking about her will.

'You know what they say – if you sort it out you won't need it,' she explained as she asked me to witness a small change she wanted to make.

And I couldn't help thinking once again of the words of that epitaph. I wondered if Doris ever thought of it. If she did, she gave no hint.

She knew of course how serious the situation was and probably in her heart she knew that her chances were very slim, yet she wanted to be positive. She wasn't afraid of dying – sorry, passing over. 'You can't die for the life of you,' as she always said. But she was afraid that she might emerge from the operation a cabbage. She desperately didn't want to be a burden on her family and she couldn't bear the thought of going into a home. She would much rather have passed on to the next world in which she believed so fervently.

And of course that's what happened. Doris didn't recover consciousness after the operation. She slipped peacefully away on May 8th 1987, less than four months after an unseen voice told her, 'Your time on earth is over . . .'

Since then a lot of things have been written about Doris that would have upset her greatly. She realized of course that a medium is always an easy target for criticism and ridicule. She knew there would always be people who disbelieved her, but she would have been horrified to see the way people who had supported her in the past turned against her when she was no longer able to defend herself.

A typical example was a well known newspaper columnist who had interviewed Doris a year or two before her death. This columnist had a reputation for being a tough interviewer with an acid tongue and Doris nervously awaited the outcome of the interview fearing that she might be ripped to shreds. Yet when the story appeared she was delighted with it.

The columnist, while confessing she was a sceptic, wrote a fair account of the meeting and included several things Doris had told her that turned out to be inexplicably correct.

Doris was so pleased with the report that she included it, with permission, in her next book.

Yet only days after Doris' death this same columnist wrote an obituary snippet in which she described the medium as an 'old fraud'.

This piece was drawn to my attention by several people and in the end I wrote to the columnist suggesting that under the circumstances it seemed rather hypocritical. She replied that I'd misunderstood her article. She didn't think Doris was a fraud, she said, in fact Doris had told her several things that led her to believe

15

there might be something in spiritualism, but she felt it was best not to meddle with such things.

Fair enough, but what a pity for Doris' memory that thousands of readers didn't have the benefit of this clarifying letter. I wonder how many other people 'misunderstood' the words 'old fraud'.

There have been many more criticisms in the past months. Doris was accused of making vast sums of money from her work. Well, I can't pretend to know the details of her financial affairs but I'm sure that she wasn't as rich as many people seem to believe. The house that was her pride and joy after a lifetime in rented accomodation was a pretty, but modest, semi-detached. The kind of two-and-a-half bedroom, 1930s house you see all over the London suburbs. The sort of house that embryo yuppies try to get away from, not aspire to.

As for the country cottage that sounded so grand – it was in fact a converted end-of-terrace chalet on a former holiday camp on the Isle of Sheppey. It was a cosy place, close to the sea and Doris was thrilled with it, but it was hardly the luxury hideaway implied in the press.

Homes apart, Doris had little on which to spend her money. She never took foreign holidays, she seldom went shopping, she didn't give lavish dinner parties and she dreaded eating in restaurants. Her only indulgence was a packet of cigarettes and a regular hair-do.

If she did receive a cheque, Doris was just as likely to give it to charity, and over the years she must have given away thousands of pounds.

Easy enough, one might say, when you have money to spare but even in the days when she was struggling to pay the rent, Doris would give what she could to those worse off than herself.

'It makes me furious when I read the terrible things that are written about Doris,' said an old friend, too shy to be named. 'I knew her long before she was a medium or anything like that and a nicer, kinder person you couldn't hope to meet. She didn't have two halfpennies to rub together in those days yet she'd give you her last penny. If ever she won anything in a raffle or at a fete, she gave it away.

'Her house was always full of people and if anyone had a problem, Doris would try to help.'

This is not to imply that Doris was a saint. She was not, as she was the first to admit. Like everybody else, Doris had her faults. She gave of her best to the bereaved, but at home, among friends, there were times when she needed to let off steam. She would have a moan now and then as she frequently confessed in her books and she was capable of being irritable when she was worried. She was only human after all. But unlike many other people, Doris sincerely tried to be good. She believed that she didn't always succeed, but she did try.

The most serious allegation made against Doris after her death was that her public demonstrations were rigged and the people who received messages were unsuspecting plants: poor bereaved souls who were invited along specially and grilled beforehand on the phone for information that Doris would later announce from the stage.

There was also a suggestion that Doris reserved the first few rows in every theatre for her plants, but this is too ridiculous to be taken seriously. Anyone who attended a Doris Stokes show will have noticed that messages were received by people seated all over the theatre. Often a recipient would have to clamber down from the balcony taking several minutes to reach the microphone. What's more, many dedicated fans followed Doris from theatre to theatre and even they would have become suspicious if, night after night, the spirits only reached the people in the front row.

The first allegation is more difficult to refute. In the last year of her life I don't think Doris could have relayed names and details back to plants in the audience even if she'd wanted to because her memory simply wasn't good enough.

What's more, having travelled with her to theatres on many occasions and having sat with her throughout the evening, either in the dressing-room or the wings, I can say that I never once saw any evidence of collusion. There were no last minute phone calls, no scribbled notes, no hurried meetings at the stage door. There was nothing to suggest that anything underhand was going on.

Nevertheless it can't be denied that Doris did sometimes invite people to her shows and she did sometimes get messages for them. As she grew more and more famous, it became impossible for her to grant all the requests for personal sittings that poured through her letter-box. Yet the letters were often heart-rending and a particularly distraught plea, accompanied by a telephone number, would frequently have Doris reaching for the phone. Without a thought for the cost she would dial all over the country at her own expense to see if she could comfort the distressed correspondent.

Somehow Doris managed to conduct a mini sitting over the telephone. Critics would say she must have milked the emotional listener for facts. Having over heard a number of these conversations, I don't agree. I never once heard Doris say to someone, 'I've got your grandmother here,' or, 'I'm talking to your father.'

She always gave a specific name or a number of identifying details as in, 'I've got an elderly man here. I think it's your grandad. He's very tall and he says he passed with cancer of the lung. It's his birthday towards the end of the month.'

Anyway, by the end of the call, Doris' surprised correspondent was usually much happier, but Doris invariably felt she hadn't done enough. Since she hadn't been able to do a full-blown sitting, she felt in some obscure way as if she'd 'short-changed' her client. So, if she was due to appear at a theatre anywhere near them in the coming months, she'd ask them to come along.

'I can't promise you'll get anything, love,' she'd say, 'but you might find it interesting to hear more about it.'

Sometimes these people would turn up and sometimes they'd get a message. Perhaps it's naïve, but given the number of people she would have talked to in the intervening weeks, I doubt very much if Doris would have remembered the relevant facts about such 'invited' members of the audience.

What's more, when she did give them messages at the theatre it was new information not previously touched on, as they often wrote and told her afterwards.

Nevertheless, knowing that there were so many critics gunning for her, it was foolish to hand them ammunition. Doris realized this, but she couldn't help herself. She was a victim of her own warm nature. She hated having to rush past the fans gathered at the stage door without a word as if she was too grand to talk to them.

'It looks as if I'm stuck up,' she'd protest to her manager, Laurie.

'Yes, but if you stop they'll say it's collusion.'

Doris saw the sense in this. Mostly she took his advice, but sometimes on her own at home with a weeping mother at the end of the phone, she weakened. And so, should the mother get a message at some later theatre demonstration the conversation could go like this:

REPORTER: Have you ever spoken to Doris Stokes before tonight?
MOTHER: Yes, she phoned me but . . .
REPORTER: And did you get a message tonight?
MOTHER: Yes but . . .
REPORTER: Thank you very much.

Open and shut case.

More difficult for the critics to explain is the fact that Doris managed to demonstrate her powers on radio phone-in programmes as well as at home in private sittings.

Doris conducted a number of mini sittings over the air at various radio stations around the country and even overseas to Australia. Whenever Doris did a radio phone-in, the phone lines were jammed and no one could pretend that she could in any way control or pre-select the callers who were put through to her. Sometimes she got in a tangle but at others the results were remarkable. On one occasion she was able to tell a caller that his daughter had been murdered. She had been strangled. Hardly a bland remark that could have applied to anyone.

As for private sittings, the critics conclude that distressed and emotional people unwittingly fed Doris the information she needed and then accepted it back again in their desperation to believe.

This is a plausible theory. Bereaved people *are* desperate to believe that their loved ones aren't gone for ever. However, the first time I met Doris she gave me a sitting. I was neither emotional nor desperate. I gave her no help or information whatsoever. I didn't even want a sitting at all. Yet she came up with some remarkably accurate details which she could not have discovered through any normal channels.

At the time, I was working as a reporter and I had been asked to write a series on the supernatural. I'd never heard of Doris Stokes. This was the late seventies and Doris was unknown outside spiritualist circles. Nevertheless the features editor had been told of a promising new medium who might have an interesting story that could be included in the series, and I was sent to talk to her.

I rang Doris out of the blue one morning to arrange an appointment.

'When d'you want to come?' asked Doris.

'As soon as possible,' I said, as all journalists do, thinking that she might say the day after tomorrow if I was lucky, or a week Wednesday if I wasn't.

'Let's see now,' said Doris. 'It's twelve o'clock now, I'm due at the hairdressers at half past and then I've got to do a bit of shopping, but I'll be back by two. Come at two.'

I was surprised to be taken so literally but two o'clock was fine with me.

I crossed London and arrived at Doris' Fulham flat just as she and her husband John were returning from the shops. John was carrying a bag of groceries and Doris was looking in her purse for her key.

She was a large woman, tall and well-built with a warm smile and particularly piercing blue eyes. She wasn't frail in those days as she later became, and she moved easily. Her thick, grey hair, obviously newly-arranged, stood out in a neatly-curled halo round her head.

We went inside and after the interview in which she outlined her remarkable life story, Doris said that she'd give me a sitting. I politely told her that this wouldn't be necessary. I had no idea what to expect but I didn't like the sound of it and I hadn't lost anyone close to me. There was no one I wanted to talk to even if it were possible, which I doubted very much.

Nevertheless, Doris insisted.

'Anyone can say they can do these things,' she said. 'I have to prove to you that I'm telling the truth.' Then without warning, she launched into an extraordinary conversation with the invisible forces which had apparently entered the room undetected by me.

It was quite unlike the eerie seances you see in the movies. Doris did not draw the curtains. She did not light candles or burn a weird red light. Neither did she fall into an alarming trance, talk in a funny voice or summon up mysterious Red Indians.

The sun continued to pour through the second-floor windows and Doris continued to sit in her leatherette armchair, smoking a cigarette and sipping a cup of tea.

If she'd been holding a receiver I would have assumed that I was overhearing a telephone conversation.

Notebook ready, I prepared to write down everything she said. I did not intend to say anything myself apart from yes or no, and I tried to clear my mind of clues. Some people said that mediums were telepathic and took their information from a client's mind. If this was true it was a pretty amazing talent anyway but nevertheless I was determined she would get nothing from me.

All the same, I couldn't prevent a strong speculation from filtering through. The only person I could think of who had recently died was my paternal grandfather who had slipped away two years before when he was in his eighties.

'I've got a man here who passed with a heart attack,' said Doris. 'Do you know anyone who had a heart attack?'

I shook my head.

'It seems quite definite,' she said, looking puzzled.

Then she started to cough – a dreadful smoker's cough from the bottom of her lungs. Doris smoked of course, but never in the years afterwards did I hear her repeat that appalling sound.

'He had a cough,' she continued, 'and I'm getting the letter M. A big letter M.'

I shook my head again. My grandfather's initial was A.

And so it went on. Most of the time the names meant nothing and I told Doris she was wrong, but I wrote it all down anyway. There were one or two striking successes however. She described several items in my home and a troublesome car which she accurately said was white. Okay, that could have been a lucky guess, but she went on to talk of a relative who had been unwell, giving her correct name – not the family name by which everyone knew her.

'There's been a lot of worry about her lately and she's been to the hospital for tests,' said Doris, 'but she's all right. The tests are clear.'

This was true except that I had no idea of the outcome of the tests. When I checked later I discovered that the results had arrived that very day. She was fine.

Amongst the unknown names, Doris also came up with names which were undoubtedly correct. People often criticized this business of apparently random names, saying that if you threw out enough common names, the subject was bound to know a few of them. This is a fair point, but Doris often came out with a sequence of names whose accuracy could not be accounted for by coincidence.

'I've got the name Wyn,' said Doris, and before I could answer that I did know this person, she went on, 'and the name Joy. Then that was Len.'

'Yes,' I said, 'I know them.'

'Now they're giving me the name Paul and, in connection with Paul, the name Clark. They're singing happy birthday to Paul so I know it's his birthday just coming or just going. He's four.'

I was amazed. Joy is a relative. Her husband's name is Len, her mother-in-law was called Wyn, her son Paul and their surname is Clark. Paul was celebrating his fourth birthday in two weeks' time.

By the end of the sitting I was thoroughly puzzled. Much had been wrong, but the things that were right were quite astonishing. You could complain that these correct details were trivial, but nevertheless they were accurate and this accuracy could not be explained by guesswork, help from me, excessive emotion on my part or clever research on Doris'. In two hours I doubt if even MI5 could have come up with so many obscure, yet correct, particulars – especially bearing in mind that Doris did not know I was married, I had given her my maiden name only, yet much of the information concerned my husband's family.

As far as I could see, the only 'logical' explanation left was telepathy – though how Doris had known the results of that hospital test before I did was a mystery.

A lucky guess perhaps?

I left the flat more confused than ever.

Two weeks later on a visit to my mother I happened to mention that I'd seen a medium.

'What did she say?' asked my mother.

'Oh, most of it was wrong,' I said, 'but there were some interesting bits.'

I happened to have my notebook with me and I began to read through the messages.

'She was going on first of all about a man who had a heart attack and a cough,' I said. 'And the letter M.'

My mother turned a little pale.

'Your grandad,' she said.

And she reminded me of what I'd forgotten. My maternal grandfather, who had died too long ago for me to remember him, had been killed by a heart attack brought on by a fit of coughing during a bout of bronchitis. His name was Martin.

What's more, many of the names which meant nothing to me, turned out to belong to great aunts and uncles I'd never heard of.

Doris had been right all along.

I was impressed.

A few weeks later I was impressed again. My feature on Doris was completed and for another part of the series I was to visit a college for psychic studies in Essex. Doris had mentioned that she knew the staff there and she offered to take me along and introduce me to them. She didn't get out much she said and it would make a nice day in the country.

We set off for Essex. The college was based in a Jacobean-style mansion surrounded by acres of beautiful parkland. I spent several hours interviewing everyone in sight while Doris renewed her acquaintance with old friends. At last, during the afternoon, I settled down in the great hall to talk to one of the students. At the other end of the hall I could see Doris sitting alone in the corner, waiting for me to finish. This was my final interview and we would be leaving afterwards.

Ten minutes later I glanced up again and noticed that Doris was no longer alone. She was deep in conversation with a man I hadn't seen before and he appeared to be recording what she was saying.

Fearing that another journalist might be embarked on the same story as me, I brought my interview to a close and went over to see what was going on.

'Hello, love,' said Doris. 'Won't be long. I had to talk to this man. I saw him walking upstairs and then I heard his wife say, "Will you have a word with my husband. He's ever so upset."'

It turned out that the man had lost his wife and since her death had been desperately looking for proof of an after-life. He had visited mediums and spiritualist churches without any luck and he had vowed that he would make one last attempt. He would spend a week at the college and if he drew a blank he would give up for ever.

That particular day was his last day and when Doris saw him he was on his way upstairs to pack.

'When she started coming out with these messages I went back for my tape-recorder,' he explained.

I sat down and Doris went on to describe his wife and the couple's only son who had died six months after his mother.

By this time the man was in tears. Silently, he took out his wallet and with a shaking hand produced a snap-shot of his departed family. The smiling faces were exactly as Doris had described.

'Now she's telling me about a special date that's important,' said Doris. 'September 26th. Is that your anniversary, love? No?' Doris turned back to the husband. 'She says no, it's more important than that.

You used to celebrate the day you met. September 26th.'

The man nodded. 'That's right. That was when we met and it always seemed more important to us than our wedding anniversary.'

There had been no prompting, no incorrect names; and the man was practically too overcome to speak, let alone provide Doris with details.

Cynics might say it could have been a set-up. I suppose it could but there was no advantage to Doris. Her feature had already been written and she knew it. What's more, if that man was acting he deserves an Oscar.

Over the next few years I was present at dozens of sittings and public demonstrations and I was constantly amazed at the things Doris would come out with. I have no doubt that she was genuine.

I have to admit that this book is biased. It is a tribute book and I haven't deliberately sought out critics and detractors. I've simply spoken to people who knew, worked with or had sittings with Doris and I've let them give their side of the story.

These people are not fools likely to be taken in by a conwoman. Neither do they have anything to gain by inventing stories.

After reading their words I doubt if even the most hardened cynic could deny that Doris Stokes had a very special gift.

Linda Dearsley
1988

The Beginning

One bright morning in the early seventies, Tom Johanson, head of the Spiritualist Association of Great Britain had a great shock.

Doris Stokes, cheerful, beaming and full of vitality, walked through the door of his office.

Not that the sight of Doris was particularly alarming – it was just that Tom had never expected to see her again. The last time they'd met, Doris had been lying in hospital on the verge of death, so ill that Tom didn't feel she would last the night.

'I was absolutely amazed when she walked in,' said Tom. 'She was so bad that I felt she wasn't long for this world. Yet she walked into SAGB headquarters in Belgrave Square a few months later, right as rain. I couldn't believe my eyes.'

Throughout her life Doris strongly believed that she was following a path laid out for her by the spirit world. Her meeting with Tom, she would have said, was fate. Certainly it was a major turning-point in her life. Had she not met Tom she might not have moved to London and put into motion the chain of events that was to make her into a household name.

Yet she could so easily have missed that first vital meeting.

Tom Johanson, as well as running the SAGB, is a reknowned healer and one weekend in the early seventies he was invited to speak at a spiritualist service at Morecambe Spiritualist Church.

'I had never heard of Doris Stokes at the time,' said Tom. 'Working at SAGB I'm obviously on the look-out for good mediums and if I hear of them I contact them, but I'd never come across Doris.

'Anyway when I arrived at Morecambe they told me that I should have been sharing the platform with one of their local mediums, Doris Stokes, but unfortunately the arrangement had had to be changed. Doris was in hospital, very ill it seemed, after an operation for breast cancer.

'Well, by this time, it was late on Saturday night so I said I'd call at the hospital the following morning to see her.

'When we finally met I must be honest and say that she looked so desperately ill I didn't think she would last the night. As a healer I'm used to seeing very sick people and Doris looked about as bad as it's possible to get.

'Yet she was very pleased to see me. "Tom," she said, "when I get well can I come and work for you at the SAGB?"

' "Of course you can," I told her. What else could I say?

'But although I said it, it was only to cheer her up and give her a bit of hope because I was so moved by her condition. I didn't seriously think she would live long enough to come to London.

' "Doris you've got a job whenever you want," I promised, never dreaming she'd take me up on it.

'Before I left she asked me to give her healing, which of course I did. And that was the end of that – or so I thought.

'Then two or three months later she walked in out of the blue. I had no idea she was coming. I had no idea she was still in this world let alone in London.

' "Well, here I am," she said, very cheerfully, "You said I could work for you," and she swore that her wonderful recovery was the result of my healing.'

Tom Johanson was faced with a dilemma. He knew nothing of Doris' work and mediums employed by the SAGB were normally expected to provide six different references from six different churches as well as go through a demonstration under test conditions in the Belgrave Square offices.

Doris did none of these things.

'I bent the rules for Doris and put her to work straight away,' said Tom. 'It wasn't that I had a gut feeling about her abilities; I can't claim any instinctive knowledge. It was simply that when we audition mediums we say, "Thank you very much, we'll call you," and I couldn't do that with Doris. She'd come through a very serious illness, she'd come a long way, she was excited and full of hope and I'd made her a promise. I couldn't go back on that. So I put her on the books then and there and she started to work.'

He also found her a flat.

'Well, Doris had come down from the North and she had nowhere to live. By chance we had a lecturer coming in once a week at that time and I happened to know that he had been left a block of flats by his father. These flats were for disabled ex-servicemen and knowing that John, Doris' husband, had been wounded at Arnhem I thought the family might qualify. I approached this man and asked if he could help. He found them a flat.'

Doris, John and their son Terry were grateful to move into the flat on the second floor of a block in Fulham. It had two bedrooms and was reasonably spacious, but it wasn't luxurious. There was no bathroom and when the family wanted a soak they used a tin bath in the kitchen. Nevertheless Doris settled down to her work at the SAGB and was glad to be in London.

'Doris worked for me for two years,' said Tom. 'I saw her work and there was one little thing which she used to do which didn't seem to me a good idea. Quite often, people are so surprised when a medium gives them a message that they can't remember all the names of the people they know. They tend to reject a name given by the medium only to remember on the way home that it was in fact correct.

'This is frustrating for the medium. Sometimes the medium is wrong, of course, but sometimes they are certain they're right. When this happened to Doris she tended, in those days, to say, "You haven't done your homework." '

'Well, that might have been true but it could look as if she was trying to shed the blame for getting something wrong, and I suggested she used a different approach.

'You see, people don't realize how difficult communication is. The link between medium and spirit is very, very tenuous and it's easy to get something wrong. I remember once being asked to help a couple who were having problems at their home in Richmond. Every night, the wife said, an invisible someone tried to pull the blankets off her in bed and she was sure they were trying to choke her.

'Well, I went along and I went into the bedroom and stood there. I didn't see anything but I got the strong impression of an old, old man lying in bed very ill.

'What are you doing to this poor lady?' I asked him mentally and I thought he replied, "She's a wrong woman."

'I got angry at that. "She's not a wrong woman," I told him. "She's a very nice person."

31

'But then I realized I'd misheard. He was trying to say, "She's the wrong woman," – a different meaning entirely.

'That's the sort of thing that can happen so easily. Then you get other cases which are very strange. I remember once the psychic artist, Coral Polge, produced a picture for a young man. She drew an old gentleman with long, bushy sideburns – a very distinguished-looking character. It was a good picture but it meant nothing to the recipient.

' "I don't know him. I haven't a clue who that is," he said.

' "He's a doctor," said Coral. "Dr Fletcher."

' "Sorry, I don't know any Dr Fletcher," said the young man.

' "He used to work at Guy's Hospital," said Coral.

'But again it made no sense to the young man and he left very unhappy. He might have complained at the waste of money but instead he decided to investigate further.

'He took the picture along to Guy's Hospital and asked for Dr Fletcher. Eventually a doctor approached. He was Dr Fletcher, he said, but he looked nothing like the picture. Nevertheless, the young man persisted. He unwrapped the portrait and showed it to the doctor.

' "I wondered if by any chance you might know him?" he asked.

' "Yes, that's my uncle. He used to work here," said the doctor. "Where on earth did you get that?"

'Now why that young man was sent along to Guy's, I don't know. Certainly, as a result of his visit the doctor became very interested in psychic phenomena so perhaps that was the reason. I believe nothing happens by accident.

'Anyway, Doris continued to work here and the reports started coming in. Every medium gets a few bad reports and so did Doris, but she also got a great many very good ones. After a while, people weren't just pleased with their sittings, they were writing us letters saying, please let us know when she's coming back. I began to realize that this lady I'd accepted out of kindness was really quite special.

'Doris was a good medium but I've known a lot of good mediums. Where Doris was different was that she was natural on the platform. Some other mediums are performers. They can't disguise that they like to be the centre of attention. But Doris would get up there and chat to people as if they were in her sitting-room. She had a lovely, grandmotherly appeal. She used to smile down benevolently and peopled warmed to that.

'Then the media took her up and the whole thing snowballed.

'She gave me the fright of my life once. She said, "Tom, let's do a two-part sort of workshop in one day. The first part in the afternoon and the second part in the evening."

'Well, the morning of the workshop I couldn't believe my eyes. There was a queue of people from the front door right to the other end of the square and the police were called. They'd been queuing since six the night before and it was chaos. Nobody could get into the other offices round here for the crowds.

'This was totally unexpected. The room only holds 180 and you can't get a quart into a pint pot. People kept coming up and saying, "I've been here since eight last night," and I'd say, "I know. I'm sorry, but I still only have 180 seats. I can't do anything about it. If you want you can sit on the stairs."

'We opened up all the doors so they could hear what Doris was saying and they sat on the stairs, but of course there was a limit to that and you're not supposed to block the exits. It was very difficult. After that we had to organize ticket-only events to keep it under control.

'One of the things I admired about Doris was the way she never forgot us at SAGB. Not mentioning any names, I have to say that many of the greatest mediums started here as nonentities. We gave them a start, we gave them publicity and all the help we could. Then they go solo, as they all want to do, and forget us. Doris was the only one who continued to come back after she became famous.

'She was very good to us. Very generous. For instance, our restaurant was looking shabby. We're a charity and funds are obviously limited. The chairs needed renewing but money was short. When Doris heard she bought us twelve beautiful tables and forty-eight beautiful chairs to match, so now our restaurant looks immaculate.'

Tom Johanson never had a sitting with Doris or any of his mediums. He doesn't feel it's necessary. The truth of his philosophy was proved to him many years ago.

'I was a sceptic as a young man,' he said. 'I was a technical writer in a laboratory. My job was to interpret the jargon of scientists and put it into simple words.

'Then my kid brother got involved in spiritualism. I was sure it was a load of rubbish. Son, I thought, it'll turn you mad. But I was curious and I went along out of curiosity. I wanted to be able to tell my brother, "You see, I've been and it's nonsense."

'I got as far as the front desk and I was standing waiting to be served when this man started talking to me. He was obviously a widely-read man and a fascinating speaker. I thought to myself, a man like that couldn't possibly be deceived. It turned out his name was Harold Sharp and he was one of the most brilliant mediums of his day.

' "Why are you here?" he asked.

' "I'm curious," I said. "I know nothing about your work but I'm sceptical."

' "Why don't you join my development class?" he asked.

'And I thought, OK, anything for experience. So I joined the class.

'I found it terribly boring at first. We had to concentrate and then each person in turn gave the impressions they were getting. When he came to me it was always, "No, Mr Sharp. Nothing."

'But there were two very attractive young women and I enjoyed the company. I carried on going for quite some time and then one day I saw something. I saw a gondola with black curtains and the water was like a piece of black glass, and as the boat moved it didn't disturb the water. It seemed very interesting to me.

' "What does that mean, Harold?" I asked.

' "It's symbolic of a funeral," he said.

'The next time I went I saw a bed at the far side of a room and in the bed was a lady, very, very ill. I couldn't see her face and mentally I went forward to look at her and the face was suddenly blanked out.

'I told Harold about it.

' "I'm afraid someone you know is going to die," he said.

'A few months later my fiancée died.

'She died on a Thursday night. I was just like a piece of senseless stone when it happened but the next day the grief got me. I just couldn't see life without her. Friday was a very bad day. So was Saturday. But on Saturday evening an old lady who lived opposite saw

35

me sitting in the corner destroying myself and she said, "Come on, young man. Let's go for a walk."

'It was very quiet and suddenly the grief dissolved and a beautiful calm came over me as if nothing had happened. I went back to my room, lay on the bed and slowly something happened. The room lit up with a fabulous light. I can't describe it, it was so bright and pure and I felt this indescribable ecstasy.

'The next day I went to the spiritualist church and the medium gave me an extraordinary message. She said that I was being prepared to bring the new philosophy into the world and that I would teach tens of thousands of people.

'It was so ridiculous that I would have burst out laughing. Yet over the years one thing led to another and now there is hardly a country in the world I haven't been to to lecture: America, Canada, Australia, China, Iceland, most countries in Europe . . . and everywhere I go there are audiences of several hundred people. So it did actually come about.'

Over the years Tom Johanson has grown accustomed to doubters.

'I think a lot of people who attack mediums or the idea of survival are afraid of it. It's something unknown which they don't understand and they are afraid. But I don't see how you can deny something you don't know about. For instance, I've never seen a flying saucer, but hundreds of people claim to have done. Now it would be stupid to say that all those people are crazy or suffering from hallucinations, so until I have concrete evidence that flying saucers don't exist, I can't attack the people who say they've seen them.

'As Professor Hyslop, a professor of Logic at Columbia University, used to say, "Any man who denies the facts about psychic phenomena denies the right to be listened to by any intelligent person.''

'We get a lot of magicians now claiming they can do what mediums do. Perhaps they can if they spend hours rehearsing and setting up gadgets, because what they do is a trick. A medium has no props, no equipment, no helpers. She just goes out on the platform and does it for real.

'Not long ago, I put a challenge to magicians in the papers. I said you pick the hall and the audience and work under the same conditions as a medium and then I'll believe you can do it.

'I've had no takers so far.'

Doris Abroad

During the late seventies and early eighties Doris travelled a great deal overseas. She visited Australia, New Zealand, the USA and Canada, and wherever she went, despite her 'difficult' Lincolnshire accent (barely discernible to British ears), she amazed believers and sceptics alike.

She demonstrated her gifts on television before some of the world's toughest interviewers; she did the same on radio phone-ins and she coped with everything the press could throw at her as if she'd been doing it all her life.

Mike Ledgerwood, at the time a British public relations officer working for a record company, accompanied Doris on some of her adventures in New York and California. It was an experience which was to change his life.

'I was doing PR work in New York and amongst other things I was promoting a soccer team. Then, out of the blue, a fat American with a fat cigar said to me: "How would you like to do publicity for this psychic I've got stashed away in London?"

'Apparently this man, who was a tour promoter, had heard of Doris' great success in Australia where she'd toured the country and filled the Sydney Opera House three times, and he hoped to do the same thing with her in the United States. He intended to have her flown to New York and he wanted someone to look after the publicity.

'I knew nothing about psychics. I'd heard of fey old ladies who read tea cups and all that sort of thing, but I'd had no personal experience at all.

' "I'll get you all the material on it and if you want to do it I'll put you in touch with her," said the fat American."

Mike Ledgerwood went away with a pile of press cuttings and by the time he'd waded through it he was intrigued. Having spent most of his working life in the record business the prospect of Doris Stokes seemed like an interesting change. He agreed to do the job.

'Doris and I spoke on the phone,' he said, 'and we arranged to meet when she arrived in New York. I think this phone conversation would have been the end of 1978 and Doris came over early in 1979.

'As it happened I was in Nashville with a band called the Fabulous Poodles, would you believe, when she arrived so I arranged for Jackie, my assistant at the record company, to meet her at the airport and take her to the Plaza Hotel while I rushed for the next plane to New York.

'I dashed straight from JF Kennedy airport to the hotel. When I got there Jackie opened the door and she was crying. I was amazed. Jackie was a tough little Jewish girl and I'd never seen her cry over anything.

'But Jackie wasn't upset. They were tears of emotion.

' "I thought I'd be prepared for anything," she said, "but this Doris Stokes . . . where did you find her?"

'And then at that moment Doris saw me. "Come in, Mike, love, and have a cup of tea," she said. "We've just been talking to Jackie's dad."

'Apparently Jackie's father had died while she was on honeymoon in Hawaii and she'd felt dreadful ever since because she wasn't there. She had no idea what

39

Doris did. When I'd asked her to meet this English lady at the airport it hadn't occurred to me to mention it.

'I'd just said something like, "This old dear is coming over from London and we're going to look after her and do a few bits and bobs. Could you take care of her till I arrive?"

'So she was completely stunned when Doris suddenly started chatting to her dad.'

Somewhat surprised himself at this dramatic beginning to their association, Mike accepted a cup of tea and sat down. In those days Doris still felt that she had to prove herself, particularly to people who were expected to work with her. This wasn't merely insecurity. At that time few people outside spiritualist circles understood what a medium did and even fewer had seen a medium work. It was therefore important, Doris felt, that people who had to represent her knew what they were talking about. So whenever she was confronted by new faces she tended to launch into a mini sitting.

'I was drinking tea and thinking that she was a nice grandmotherly figure, oozing kindness and consideration,' said Mike, 'but that it would be a real hard job to get her exposure in New York – it's not an easy city –when all of a sudden she started popping a few things from spirit.

'I was very close to a guy called Rick Wakeman at that time, a pop star who was on AM records. I'd been with him in New York and he'd just left for a vacation in the Bahamas. Anyway, Doris started talking about a Richard or a name like Richard and telling me various things about him.

'Then it all came out of that. From there she started on family details and then she came up with an old family friend from way back before the sixties. I hadn't thought of him for years but suddenly she was picking up this name: "Ernest. No, it's not Ernest, there is a foreign accent. Ernst."

'This was a guy I'd known as a kid in England. He'd died in a boating accident in Austria and she knew all about the tragedy and everything.

'Well, hearing is believing, and after that I began to take an interest in psychic things. What's more, far from having trouble getting coverage for her, the whole thing just snowballed. Television and radio shows – the response was overwhelming. I was amazed. There wasn't so much in print but the talk shows were back-to-back and the phone rang so much it was falling off the wall.

'Doris, bless her, when she got a desperate case would say, "If you want to get in touch with me, luvvy, ring this number," and she'd give my answer-service number over the air. I'd get home later and the woman would say, "I've had 370 calls for you today. I'll have to put your rate up. Anyway, who is this Doris Stokes?"

' "You'd better come and see her at the theatre and then you'll understand why you got the calls," I told her.'

Unfortunately for the tour promoter the media interest didn't translate into large earnings.

'He decided to pull out,' said Mike. 'He couldn't make money fast enough. For instance he turned down the David Suskind show – the New York equivalent of the Johnny Carson show, or, in a smaller way, Wogan over here – because there was no big fee.

'Well, I thought that was a great shame. So did Doris. So I got together with a friend of mine, Bill Sissplatt, and we decided to put our money together and bring Doris back later in the year.'

At this stage Mike Ledgerwood was still immersed in a public relations career with no serious thought of changing direction. He was no more interested in murder investigations than anyone else. And yet, shortly before Doris was due in New York for the second time, a baffling missing-child case caught his eye.

'This was probably the biggest missing-child story New York had seen for years. A small boy of six named Etan Patz had apparently disappeared on his way to the school bus. The police suspected they had a murder on their hands but no body was discovered. Anyway, the case was huge. There were big coloured posters everywhere, which you don't often see in New York. Not concerning missing children anyway.

'I knew how strongly Doris felt about children so I arranged for her to talk to the parents by phone from England. Well, she came up with all this information that was correct and naturally the parents wanted to meet her face-to-face when she came to New York, so I arranged that too.'

The meeting at the Patz's New York apartment went well. Doris came up with many names and details that were accurate. She also felt that she spoke to Etan himself but she didn't like to say that it was definitely him. She never forgot the shock she suffered during the war when a medium told her that her missing husband was dead – when in fact he was lying severely wounded in hospital.

Now that she was a medium herself she dreaded making a similar mistake and putting anyone else through such a trauma. Nevertheless, privately, she thought that the boy had been killed.

'Doris came out with all this information,' said Mike. 'I investigated it myself, checked names and addresses and wrote to the cops. She was very hot on that case. So hot, I think that the police were embarrassed.'

42

But then, inexplicably, things went wrong. During her first telephone conversation with the parents, Doris had named a sweetshop known to Mrs Patz as a favourite haunt of her son. Doris felt that the area surrounding this shop was highly significant to the boy's disappearance, and once she arrived in New York it was suggested she visit the street in the hope of picking up some 'vibes'.

The press got to hear of the scheme and turned up as well which sadly upset the parents.

'We were in Greenwich Village and the mother came after us like a banshee,' said Mike. 'It was really weird. "What are you doing down here?" she said. "Don't you know they might fly the coop?"

'It struck me as a strange thing to say. Anyway, she made it clear that she didn't want us involved in the case any more. It had all got out of hand.

'Doris was upset about it but she was very busy. She did the David Suskind show after all.

'Suskind was a real hardnosed sceptic but she turned him upside-down. He makes a rule that he never sees anybody before he meets them on the show but Doris did a sitting for the producer and then she did the same for Suskind on the phone. After that they bent the rules of the show. They didn't normally have a live audience but they got one for Doris. The show normally lasted forty-five minutes but they let it run for an hour and a half.

'There were amusing moments, too. At one point a woman stood up to ask a question. "Mrs Stokes," she said, "You obviously believe in ESP?" '

' "Yes, luvvy," said Doris, "Extra-sensory conception." '

'Everybody just fell about.

43

'By this time there was tremendous interest in Doris and I was like a star myself because she was with me. The record company girls were queuing up for private readings and they'd leave the hotel dabbing a handkerchief to their eyes. Five minutes later, they'd phone me up saying, "This woman is incredible. How did you find her?"

'By now Bill and I had got into a routine. Knowing how good Doris was with murder cases we wanted to make sure that she couldn't get any details from the papers that might influence her. Every morning we went through the papers before she saw them and cut out anything that we felt might spark her off. Often when she picked up a paper to read it Doris would find a big hole in the middle of the page, which must have been annoying. But she went along with this. She wanted to be sure that, no matter what any critics said, we knew she was genuine and that anything she did say was therefore valuable.

'The other part of the routine was more simple. I carried a loaded tape-recorder everywhere we went because I never knew when Doris would pop out with something amazing.'

This proved to be particularly useful when Doris was invited to Los Angeles to appear on a TV show.

'While we were there,' said Mike, 'Doris was invited to the Polo Lounge in Beverly Hills to have tea with a TV-soap actress called Kay Stevens. Kay wanted a sitting but she also wanted to put on a good tea for Doris. She brought her own silver tea-service along and there was Earl Grey or whatever to drink.

'Doris and John were all agog. It was very Hollywood with quite a few famous faces around, and they were enjoying themselves.

'Anyway, there were about six of us at the table and the conversation was flowing when all of a sudden, right in the middle of a sentence, Doris said, "Who's gone missing? Who's got a Rolls Royce?"

'Now this was about 2.45 on Saturday afternoon. Quickly I switched on my tape-recorder and got down what Doris said.

'She mentioned the names Vic and Rose, a maroon-and-white Rolls Royce and the fact that this man had been shot twice in the head. There was also the name of a suspect.

'It meant absolutely nothing to me. Kay thought at first that Doris must be referring to a murder that had occurred in Beverly Hills some years before. This turned out to be a red herring. The names and details didn't fit.

'Knowing how right Doris usually was, Bill and I went to the police in Beverly Hills. That was wrong; they knew nothing about it. So then we went downtown to the missing persons bureau, but in America when it's concerning an adult they don't want to know unless the person's been missing more than forty-eight hours.

'Now I'm a junky for newspapers – I like to keep abreast of things – and I hadn't seen anything about any missing people. The next day, Sunday, Doris and John went to see some English friends up in the Hollywood Hills. I'd already read the papers. Once again there was nothing about any missing people.

'I was frustrated because I wanted to find out what this weird business of Vic, Rose and the Rolls Royce was all about but I couldn't seem to get anywhere.

'Anyway, we ran Doris and John to their friends' home and afterwards I went back to my room to monitor the radio while Bill sat by the pool with his feet

45

in the water reading the sports page for the Dodgers result.

'Suddenly, as I was in my room, I heard this great shout from the pool side: "Holy Mackerel!"

'I rushed out and there was Bill holding up the sports section of the *LA Times*. He'd found a story about a missing sports promoter. His name was Vic Weiss, his wife was called Rosemary and he owned a 'red' Rolls Royce.

'We knew we were on to something then.

'This time I insisted that the PR spokesman for the LA Police Department called us at the hotel. It was like a TV drama.

' "Right," I said, "I want you to look at your watch. I make it 9.45 p.m. and I want to tell you something that Mrs Stokes told us because I think you should know it now and you should put it down on record because I don't want to read it three days later in the papers."

' "Okay," he said, "be down-town tomorrow at ten."

'After that the story unfolded day by day. The body of Vic Weiss was found in his Rolls Royce which had been left in a carpark. At first they weren't sure how he was killed and the papers described the car as 'red' but later they confirmed that the Rolls was in fact maroon-on-white just as Doris had described. She was right, too, about the two shots that had killed him.

'She had done so well that we went up to the scene of the crime – the carpark where the body had been found in the back of the car – to see if Doris could get anything else. She tuned in and after a while she said, "I think, my dear, I think I've got him through."

'Then she said something strange. "Don't take me under, luvvy. They won't know what to do."

'Afterwards I asked her what she meant by this and she explained that Vic was coming in so close and so

46

strong that she would have taken on his features and Bill and I wouldn't know what to do. She was right. It would have freaked us out.

'Doris came out with more names and details including the fact that Weiss was found with his hands tied behind his back, his knees up and his shoes off. None of these things had been printed, yet they all turned out to be correct.

'In recent years the LA police have tried to deny that they were interested in Doris' information or that they took extensive notes of what she had to say, or even that she was of any help at all. Yet I was there. I took the tape along. I played it in the Commander's office and I was translating Doris' Midlands accent so that they could understand it.

'There were two journalists present, as well as at least two other policemen, and they all took notes.

'Afterwards one of the journalists who'd been present came to the hotel to have tea with Doris. He was very close to the police and he told us that they were working from her information but, as they'd already warned me: "The Los Angeles Police Department policy is to never admit that a psychic has helped us. It was a catch-22 situation. Whatever Doris did she was not going to get any credit for it.

'But strange things started happening in California. Doris got a lot of publicity over the case and suddenly strange people in dark glasses with sallow complexions started turning up at the hotel. There was something ominous about it. I mean, there are a lot of people like that in California and they all wear dark glasses, but this one in particular had a car with a Nevada number plate.

' "Don't worry, love, they won't hurt us," said Doris, but I must confess that I was a little intimidated and we changed hotels until it was time for them to fly home.'

With Doris gone, Mike found himself thinking more and more about her uncanny powers with murder cases. In addition to the Vic Weiss and Etan Patz episodes he had also witnessed the strange and macabre events surrounding Doris' involvement with a witchcraft murder in which a small boy had been hanged in New York.

'The detective in the Bronx had most of the information he needed but there were still a few details that were unclear. He'd seen Doris on TV or something and he thought she might be able to help, so he asked her to go down to the police station.

'Doris wrote about it in *More Voices in My Ear*. As far as I was concerned I just put a tape on the filing cabinet and waited outside while Doris sat with the mother for about one and a half hours. I thought no more about it till I got home that night and John phoned.

' "I think you'd better get over here," he said, "Doris isn't very well."

'I thought, oh dear, red alert, and I rushed over to the hotel in a cab. When I got to their room Doris was very shaky and she was sitting in her dressing-gown.

' "Look at this lot," she said. She pulled down the neck of her dressing-gown and there was a deep red welt round her neck.

'Nobody believes me when I tell them this but I saw it myself and it gave me the creeps. The boy had been hanged and the mark on Doris' neck was just where the wire would have cut into his skin.'

The more Mike thought about it the more convinced he became of Doris' accuracy. In particular, he was fascinated by the Vic Weiss case. The police seemed to be getting nowhere yet Mike was sure that the Doris Stokes tape contained vital clues. Piece by piece, he began following up the leads in his spare time until in the end the case was demanding so many hours that he gave up his public relations job to become an investigative journalist.

Gradually he came across information that made him realize the Vic Weiss case was only a small part of a much bigger story.

'It has consumed my life ever since,' said Mike. 'It's taken a long time but slowly the jigsaw pieces have fitted together and I will shortly be publishing my own book on the story. I owe Doris a lot. The extraordinary thing is that, eight years later, things she said that didn't mean anything at the time, are all falling into place.

'In particular, she mentioned a name which made no sense then. Now I realise that it's the name of a man who figures very strongly in the case. He's the "Mr Big", if you like.

'I'd never have dreamed back in 1979 that Doris' information could be significant eight or nine years later, but that just shows how good she was. She changed my career and she changed my life. I think I'm a better person now because of her influence. She made me understand a lot about things I hadn't previously bothered to consider.

'We worked her very hard and I must share a bit of the guilt for that, but she wanted to do it. That was the trouble. There would be a talk show and a phone-in. Then it was, "We want you back tomorrow, Doris. Can you be here at midnight?" and Doris always said yes. She put herself through it and it took its toll.

'I've a lot to thank Doris for. A lot of people have. Once you've been touched by Doris Stokes you never forget it.'

Doris At Home

NANCY SHEEN

The first time Nancy Sheen called on Doris at her home in Fulham, she put her head round the open front door, unsure whether she should barge in uninvited.

'It's all right, Nance. Come in!' Doris called cheerfully from the kitchen. 'Your Fred tells me you've got his socks on!'

And Nancy was rather taken aback, as well she might be. She hadn't told Doris that her late husband was called Fred and there was no way anyone else could have known that, that morning, feeling rather chilly, she'd slipped into a pair of Fred's old socks before leaving home.

'I never had a sitting as such with Doris,' said Nancy, 'but over the years she gave me some wonderful evidence. Once, when she wasn't very well, she came out with some marvellous things quite spontaneously.

'It was a Saturday afternoon and Doris was poorly with an abscess on the head. She always had something, poor darling. Anyway, John had gone shopping. I changed the dressing on her head and then I made us a cup of tea. We took our cups into the sitting-room to be more comfortable and we were sitting there having a cigarette when all of a sudden Doris said to me: "D'you know I've got your mum and dad here?"

' "Have you?" I said.

' "Yes," said Doris. "You've never told me your father's name and now I know why."

' "Why?" I asked.

' "It's Jonah," she said, " and your mother is Kate."

'This was quite right, and I'd deliberately never told anyone my father's name because it was so unusual; I knew that if a medium did ever get it right she couldn't be guessing.

' "Your mother doesn't speak like you, she's a Cockney," Doris went on, "and your father is a North Country man."

' "That's right," I said.

' "And I've got your Auntie Mary here . . ." Doris went right through my family in the spirit world, naming them all, even my grandma.

' "I don't know why they're here, Nance, they haven't told me," she said.

'It was quite incredible, but there was one thing that puzzled me. Only one member of my family hadn't come forward to say hello and that was my Uncle Jim. Now Uncle Jim was only fourteen years older than me and we were very great friends. I couldn't think why he should be left out.

'I knew enough about mediums and the way they work to know that you can't pick and choose who comes to speak to you though, and I was very pleased with the message so I said nothing about Uncle Jim.

'Anyway, John came back from the shops, I went home and I thought no more about it.

'The next morning about nine o'clock the phone rang. It was John.

' "Would you mind coming down Nance?" he asked. "Doris isn't at all well."

' "Don't worry love," I said. "I'll be right down. I'll cook the Sunday lunch for you."

'I'd just put the phone down when it rang again. John tended to be a bit forgetful so I was sure he'd forgotten something.

51

' "What d'you want now, John?" I asked. "What did you forget to tell me?"

' "How did you know it was John, Nance?" asked a strange voice.

'That brought me up short. "Which John are you?"

' "I'm your cousin Maureen's husband," he said. "I'm afraid I've got to tell you that Auntie Vi died in the middle of the night. About two or three in the morning she went out to the loo and had a heart attack in the bathroom. Maureen thought you'd want to know straight away."

'I thanked him for being so thoughtful. We didn't chat long because he had a lot of other calls to make but I put the phone down thinking what a strange coincidence it was. I'd been thinking of Uncle Jim, and Auntie Vi was Uncle Jim's wife.

There was nothing I could do so I carried on as planned. I got myself ready and went down to Doris. She was sitting in the kitchen when I arrived, looking very poorly, but before I could say a word she held up a finger to stop me speaking.

' "I've got your Uncle Jim here," she said." He didn't come to see you yesterday with the rest of the family because he was waiting for his wife who passed to the spirit world in the early hours of this morning."

'I was amazed. That was the finest evidence I've ever heard from anyone.'

Nancy Sheen, joint vice-president of Fulham Spiritualist Church was Doris' best friend. They met eight or nine years ago when they were both living in the same block of flats in Fulham and from then until the day Doris died, they spoke almost every day.

'I'd heard of Doris through the church,' said Nancy, 'but we hadn't met, even though we lived in the same block of flats, because we lived on different floors.

'Anyway, one afternoon I was out on the balcony and I saw Doris and John coming along. John was holding Doris' arm and helping her walk. She'd just come out of hospital and was trying to get back on her feet again.

' "Hello Doris," I said. "How are you?"

' "Not too bad, love," she said. "You must be Nancy."

' "That's right."

' "I could see you were one of us as soon as you came towards me," she said. "I could see your aura."

'We chatted for a bit and then Doris went back but a few days later John came and knocked at my door. He explained that Terry was at work and he had to go out and he didn't want to leave Doris on her own. Would I mind going and sitting with her if I wasn't too busy?

'So I went downstairs to sit with Doris and of course we chatted on and on like the two old women we were. After that she always wanted me there and I wanted to be there and that's how we became friends. We were so close, people used to think we'd known each other twenty or thirty years.

'I thought she was lovely. She was kind and caring. That very first day when I went in they were finishing their porridge; they always had porridge, they were never ones for bothering about bacon and eggs even when they stayed in hotels.

'There were carrier bags of mail all over the kitchen and Doris was opening letters and crying her eyes out. Porridge and tears was what Doris had for breakfast every morning.

' "Look at this one, Nancy," she'd say. "Isn't it dreadful?"

'And she'd show me some heart-rending letter from someone asking for help.

53

' "I wouldn't know how to answer that, Doris," I used to say. "How do you know what to say?"

' "The spirit world gives me the answer," she'd say.

'She had a great sense of humour. One Sunday she phoned to ask if I was taking the chair at Fulham Church that night.

'I told her I wasn't.

' "In that case could you chair for me?" she asked.

' "Of course, Doris," I said, thinking that she must be visiting some church.

' "Have you got an evening dress?"

' "Yes," I replied.

' "Well, put it on. I'm wearing mine," said Doris.

'Even then it didn't strike me as strange. A lot of mediums are very poor and tend to be a bit shabby but they try to keep one good dress for platform appearances and it's quite usual to wear a long dress for special church evenings.

'So I put on my evening dress and we drove off to somewhere on the other side of London. It was a horrible night, dark and dreary, and we arrived at the back door of this building and hurried inside. We were shown into a sort of ladies cloakroom and we said a little prayer together, just as we used to before a church service.

'A few minutes later, somebody called out: "Come on! It's time!"

'And we hurried along the corridor. Out in front I could hear a loudspeaker announce: "Here's Nancy Sheen from Fulham Spiritualist Church."

'So I walked through the door and I nearly collapsed. I was on a stage and looking down at hundreds of people. Worse still the microphone was right at the other side of the stage and I had to walk across in front of all those faces. I shook like a leaf and my knees were actually knocking together as I walked, but I made it and I hung on to the microphone to stop me falling over.

'Goodness knows what I said. I rabbited on and then I heard myself saying, "Ladies and gentlemen, will you please welcome the lady with the voices in her ear – Doris Stokes!"

'And Doris came on and did her bit. It turned out to be a lovely evening but I don't remember too much about it!

'Afterwards Doris laughed and laughed. She knew that I could do it really but she was afraid that if she'd told me I wouldn't have the confidence to say yes. We laughed all the way home in the car.

'After that I chaired dozens of meetings for Doris and I often went on tour with her.

'Doris always produced wonderful evidence and she worked hard to make sure it went to the right person. I remember once she was talking to a lady and she said, "I'm getting a parrot here and he's saying, 'Who's a pretty boy then?' "

'Of course, everybody laughed and the woman said, "Yes, that's right, we used to have a parrot and he always said that."

'Another medium might have left it at that but Doris shook her head.

' "No, sorry, love. That's not right. It's Mr Parrot, not a pet parrot, they're telling me."

'And another lady sitting close by jumped up.

' "Yes!" she said, "I know a Mr Parrot and he used to say 'Who's a pretty boy then!' It was his joke."

'The message was for her.

'After a demonstration, Doris took a long time to come down to normal again. Back home, the first thing she wanted was a cup of tea and she'd sit and shed tears over the people she'd seen that night and their terrible problems.

'She didn't remember everything, of course, but the harrowing stories stuck in her mind. That poor woman whose son had been killed on a motorbike, or that poor man whose wife had committed suicide. She would be really upset for them. On the other hand, she was very happy for youngsters who were thrilled to bits to have talked to their mum or their dad. She was uplifted by that sort of case because she'd given them a bit of happiness.

'We had a lot of laughs as we travelled about the country. One January evening we went to Ipswich where Doris was doing a TV programme. They sent a rough old mini-cab for us and on the way home the driver got lost.

' "I'll be all right once I find Colchester," he kept saying, "I know my way from there."

'For some reason he wouldn't go on the motorway. He seemed nervous of it. Anyway we finally reached Colchester about seven o'clock but it turned out that he wasn't all right at Colchester. His navigating was just as bad between Colchester and London as it had been between Ipswich and Colchester!

'It was dark and cold and pouring with rain and we seemed to be going round in circles. We didn't get home till nearly midnight.

'Everybody was a bit upset but suddenly I saw the funny side and I started to laugh. Doris looked at me and then she started to laugh, and once we started we couldn't stop. We giggled like a couple of kids all the way up to the flat.

'It had been a funny day altogether. Doris had been trying to make the television programme for a director who didn't seem to have any idea how she worked. He thought she could stop and start like an actress saying her lines.

'Doris would tune in and start to come out with a message and he'd say, "Cut! Cut! Can we do that again."

'Well, Doris couldn't just say to whoever she was talking to, hold on a minute will you say that again?

'I jumped up once and said, "You can't do this. It's impossible!"

'But he carried on interrupting Doris and spoiling things until in the end one of the huge lights crashed down off its stand, missing John by inches.

'That's it. That's the spirit world warning you," said Doris.

'He was a bit subdued at first after this but gradually he went back to interrupting again until in the middle of one of his interruptions all the lights went out.

'The engineers went over everything but they couldn't find any fault. As far as we were concerned it was the spirit world getting its own back.

'Little things like that happened all the time. There were also more down-to-earth incidents that made us laugh.

'Doris never minded talking about her mastectomy operation and the fact that she wore a false boob, as she called it. She used to joke about it but really it was quite uncomfortable. Doris was a big lady and her false boob was filled with oil and therefore very heavy. On stage she used to get very hot and the first thing she wanted to do when she got home was take her boob off.

'Well, one day we were getting ready to leave our hotel in Birmingham for the trip back to London after a tour. We were packing the last things in the case and I said to Doris, "Don't put that boob on, love. You're going straight down to the car and then to your own home. Why not be comfortable?"

'As it turned out Doris already had the boob on but she went and took it off.

'The car came, we collected up our bits and hurried out, not realising that in the rush we'd left the boob behind!

'Doris didn't miss it but the next day the hotel phoned to say they'd found her boob under the bed. Well, we were in stitches over that.

'We had a lot of laughs about silly things because Doris was just an ordinary, everyday lady. She liked her soap operas and Catherine Cooksons just like everyone else. I think that's why she was so popular. There was no side with her. She was a down-to-earth lady and she liked a giggle, but she wouldn't hurt anybody willingly. I've never known her say anything hurtful to anybody. She would always be charming to them even if they were nasty to her.

'Sometimes we'd get born-again Christians outside the theatre and they'd say, "You're in league with the Devil."

' "I've never met him, love," she'd reply; "You must have met him if you know him. I don't."

'In other places they'd shout that they were praying against her.

' "Well that's not very Christian, is it, love?" she'd say quietly. "Surely you ought to be praying for me, not against me."

'She always had good answers for them. Yet she wasn't an extra clever lady. She wasn't educated. She must have got her answers from the spirit world.

'She was always kind and she would always put her hand in her pocket. She couldn't bear to see a child in the newspaper that hadn't had a Christmas present,

58

and she would do something about it. It was the same with that little dog, Boots. She saw a photograph of him in the paper and she had to give him a home.

'She was always willing to give. It was open house for friends anytime. When you walked in, it was, "Put the kettle on, love. Have you had anything to eat?" You could have had anything she'd got. She'd never think of tomorrow. If you needed it today, you could have it. I think she'd been like that all her life.

'I remember after we came back from her fortieth wedding anniversary party we brought all these presents back in the car. There were lots of presents. Doris changed out of her smart dress into something more comfortable, made a cup of tea and settled down to open the parcels.

'I was sitting there and she said, "Didn't reach your fortieth, did you, Nance?"

' "No," I said, "My husband died just before our thirty-ninth anniversary."

' "Never mind, love," said Doris. "Share ours. Undo some of these presents. They could have been for you. Come on. Undo some of these."

'And we sat there, tearing into the gifts, surrounded by paper. Not many people would have been as thoughtful as that.

'Doris was thrilled with each and every gift as if she'd never had a present before. It didn't matter what its value. She had so many things – like an artificial rose, or a little knick-knack someone had given her. Over the years they got old and shabby but she wouldn't throw them away or move them.

'There were things on her sideboard that were a bit tatty but she wouldn't hear of them being put into a drawer.

' "No," she would say, "That was given with love, and I must keep it."

'As for children, she was so pleased if a child sent her a little thing he'd made, you'd have thought she'd been given an expensive cut-glass vase.

'Sometimes, sentimental people sent her money to buy flowers for her spirit children. These were spirit children she'd spoken to during sittings with their parents. Afterwards the parents often sent Doris photographs of the child and Doris put them on a special board she'd had made. Every day, fresh flowers were put out beside the board for the spirit children, regardless of the cost and regardless of whether a donation had been left or not.

'The board got bigger and bigger, yet she knew every child on it and there were so many. Look at little Michelle or little Joseph or whatever, she'd say, what a beautiful child. She knew every one.

'The great thing about Doris was that she brought people so much comfort. We've all been bereaved and it takes a long time to get over a bereavement. Everybody has lost someone. It might not be someone very close when you are young, but as you get older they get closer, and you are left behind. Suddenly you've got a lot of family and friends in the spirit world and bereavement takes a lot of living with. It takes a long, long time.

'That's where Doris could help. At public demonstrations she would give people little messages that eased the pain, and those that didn't get messages could relate to those who did.

'People would say, why would the spirit world send back all these unimportant details like buying a new cooker or mentioning a special holiday you had as a child.

'What they don't realize is that you don't want to hear the meaning of existence. You just want proof that loved ones are still there, involved in your life.

'The other day, I was chairing a meeting and the medium insisted on giving me a message.

' "I've got two gentlemen here, they are both friends of yours and they are laughing about your shoes. Why are they laughing about your shoes? They look perfectly good red shoes to me."

'And I had to laugh myself. "I'll tell you," I said. "These shoes came from the bring-and-buy stall downstairs. My feet were aching today and I said to Lou, who runs the stall, 'You haven't got a pair of shoes that would fit me, have you, Lou? My feet are killing me.'

' "These are the shoes she gave me!"

'It was only a silly little message but it meant a lot to me. It showed that my friends were around and joking with me from the spirit world, just as they would have done if they'd been on earth.'

When Doris moved to South London Nancy was unable to drop in as frequently as before. Nevertheless she usually made the journey once a week and they spoke every day on the phone.

Then, on April 5th last year, Nancy arrived at the pretty blue-and-white house that was Doris' pride and joy and was shocked when Doris opened the door.

'She looked dreadful,' said Nancy, 'I've never seen anyone look so ill in my life. I knew then that she wasn't going to live for very much longer.

'Her skin was tight and shiny and she looked exhausted.

'I couldn't say that, of course, so I just said, "What've you been doing to yourself, love?"

' "Oh, I've just had a massage," said Doris, mistaking my meaning, "I always feel wonderful after a massage."

'She looked very ill but she was appearing at Lewisham Theatre the next night and she was determined to go through with it.

'She did manage the show but I was told afterwards that they'll never know how they managed to get her on to the platform. Apparently it was a wonderful evening. I think it was the last show she ever did.

'She went into hospital shortly afterwards. I knew all along that she wasn't going to get better this time. It was very sad. It's better not to know these things, I think.

'I miss her very much, of course. I miss those daily phone calls. What we found to gossip about, I can't think, but I miss it.

'But I shouldn't feel sad for Doris. She just went to sleep, which is the way she would have wanted it, and now I'm sure she's meeting all those loved ones and all those spirit children that she so wanted to see.'

PAT BUTTEN

As she became more famous and the stress inevitably built up, Doris began to long for a break. She had her own pretty home at last but she was suprised to discover that being in her beloved house wasn't quite the same as being on holiday.

Even when the sun shone and she could sit in the garden surrounded by her favourite roses, the phone never stopped ringing, the endless tragic letters never stopped pouring through the letter-box and, being Doris, she was quite unable to ignore them.

It was obvious that she could only rest if she got right away altogether. The problem was where to go.

Hotels had lost their charm after weeks of every year spent touring the country. Besides, it had reached the stage where Doris' face was so well known that people recognized her wherever she went, and in any public place she was approached by the eager and the desperate, the light of hope shining clearly in their eyes. Each one hated to disturb Doris but was quite convinced that theirs was a special case, as she would realize if she could just spare a minute to listen.

Doris found it almost impossible to turn such people away but she couldn't work all the time. The only solution, it seemed, was her own little retreat. Somewhere where she could sniff the sea air undisturbed, without having to travel for hours to get there.

She found what she was looking for on the Isle of Sheppey, a short drive from her home on the South London, Kent border. The owners of a former holiday camp were renovating the chalets and selling them off to create a private holiday village complete with its own swimming pool, bar and restaurant facilities. The place, in its early stages, bore a faint resemblance to a disused airfield but it was friendly, unpretentious and only a few minutes from the sea.

Doris visited the site and was pleased with what she saw. The park would be lovely when it was finished, she could tell, and the single-storey, pebble-dashed, end-of-terrace cottage she was shown had its own little garden at the back, a bright living-room, modern bathroom and two comfortable bedrooms. It was absolutely ideal, she thought.

Doris had great plans. She would get herself a bathing costume and swim every morning in the indoor pool – early when there was no one about so she wouldn't have to worry about her boob. She would stroll on the beach, picnic in the countryside . . . It would all be so different.

In fact she did none of these things but she enjoyed the cottage nevertheless. Doris just couldn't help taking her way of life with her wherever she went, and she imported a modified version to her Sheppey retreat. Soon the bereaved were drinking tea on her chintz sofa. A new set of friends was calling in for a chat, and somehow the phone – Doris never could manage without a phone – rang constantly despite the secret number.

Doris never did even get as far as the sea.

Yet it didn't matter. The sea breezes found their way into her tiny garden where they were just as beneficial, she was sure, as they would have been on the beach. And she slept more soundly in her cottage than anywhere else. Sheppey was a success.

It wasn't long before a magnificent seascape in oils appeared on the living-room wall. Anyone else would have chosen it quite deliberately to emphasize the nautical flavour of the place. This was, after all, a cottage by the sea even if you couldn't actually see the waves. But such an idea wouldn't have occurred to Doris. Her walls were not for underlining atmosphere, they were for displaying gifts.

The picture could just as easily have been a still life or a child's purple-and-orange interpretation of 'Granny Doris'. It was just happy chance that a grateful reader and Sheppey neighbour should turn out to be a talented marine artist.

'I lost my daughter Sally when she was only twenty-one,' said Pat Butten. 'She was a beautiful girl. She fell from the top of a multi-storey carpark. I'd read Doris' books before I lost her and they were a great help at a difficult time. My husband is an artist and when we heard that Doris was coming to Sheppey we sent one of his seascapes to the cottage with a note thanking Doris for the comfort her books had given us and adding that we hoped she would enjoy the picture.'

Doris, of course, was thrilled with the painting and telephoned Pat immediately to thank her.

'Doris was very kind and friendly and asked if I'd like to go over for a cup of tea,' said Pat. 'When I got to the cottage there was another couple already there.

' "You've lost a daughter," said Doris when I walked in. "I know because this lady's daughter has just brought her in," and she indicated the other woman. It was odd but this other child had been mentally handicapped and my Sally worked with the mentally handicapped so she would have had a natural affinity with the little girl.

'I hadn't expected a sitting but Doris seemed to have my Sally there. "She fell from a height, she's telling me." said Doris. "Who's Georgina?" Now Georgina is my other daughter who's now twelve – there was a thirteen year gap between them.

' "Sally's sister," I explained.

' "And she's saying something about Pat. Who's Pat?" asked Doris.

'This was extraordinary because, although my name is Patricia, most people call me by my middle name which is Anne and I'd introduced myself to Doris as Anne. She has no idea that Pat was anything to do with me.

' "That's my real name," I said, and from then on Doris called me Pat because that's what Sally had told her.

' "Sally's talking about Debbie and Julie," said Doris.
' "They're her friends."

' "And she says Georgina's been a bridesmaid recently and the bridesmaid's dress is still hanging in her wardrobe."

'This was quite true. Georgina had been a bridesmaid to Debbie not long before.

'I went to the cottage quite often after that and when Doris wasn't there I kept an eye on things for her. She was a lovely lady. She was always telling me funny little stories. I remember once she was reminiscing about her nursing days and she mentioned a doctor they used to nickname 'Knobs' because he was so obsessed with hygiene that he even covered the doorknobs so that he wouldn't pick up germs left there by other people.

'Doris loved to talk and she loved company. She was supposed to be resting but if the weather was fine she would be out in the garden chatting over the fence.

'Georgina loved her. She called her Auntie Doris and Doris often came out with little things from Sally for her.

' "Sally's telling me that sausages are your favourite," she'd say. (True.) Or, "Sally's telling me that Maths is your worst subject." (True.)

'Georgina accepted this as quite natural. She didn't think it strange at all.

'Doris was always so generous; the first Christmas we knew her she gave us a beautiful camera. She never forgot Georgina's birthday and she was always giving her little treats.

'I don't think there'll ever be another medium like Doris. Even my husband, George, who had been sceptical before he met her was given details that helped. He was very fond of Doris and said she was a lovely, genuine lady.

'She gave so much comfort. Some people think that she must have done it for gain. They think everything is for money. But Doris just wasn't like that. What she had, she gave away.

'It's such a shame she had her cottage for so short a time. She would ring me up and say she wanted to come down, but something always seemed to happen to prevent her.'

During her last illness Doris was convinced that if she could only get down to Sheppey, the sea air would work its usual magic and she would be well. Sadly, it wasn't to be. The trip could not be fitted into her busy schedule and by the time she had a space in her engagements she was too ill to travel.

After her death, Pat was inspired to write a poem which summed up her feeling about Doris. She asked if it could be included in this book along with a poem by her daughter Sally which Doris had promised to publish.

Tribute to Doris

God knows the grief that mothers feel,
The pain that never heals
When our little ones return to him
He knows just how it feels.
He didn't want the suffering that losing them
    provokes,
So to ease our pain and sorrow he gave us Doris
    Stokes.
She gently taught us those we love are always
    close at hand,
She proved it with her messages from the spirit
    land.
She gave so freely all she had to children here on
    earth,

Money and possessions for her had little worth.
Now God has called to Doris,
Her work on earth is done,
She'll be greeted by our little ones
And her beloved son.
God has taken Doris
To free her from her pain,
We love and miss you Doris
But our loss is Heaven's gain.

Pat Butten

The Child on the Marsh

Who is the child who's been seen on the
    Marsh?
Is he a long lonely soul from the past?
His sad haunted eyes that don't ever cry
Tell a tale of pain from decades gone by.
Where have his Mother and Father gone?
To a land far away but it seems he's stayed on.
Why and nobody knows
But a love once so deep in his eyes clearly
    shows.

Sally Butten

The Celebrities

DEREK JAMESON

'I didn't know Doris Stokes and I don't know if you knew her,' wrote one of Derek Jameson's perplexed fans, 'but I've got a message from her for you. She says, "Poor old Derek. He doesn't know if he's on his arse or his elbow!"

'Please excuse the language. I don't know if she would have spoken like that, but that's the message I've got to give you.'

And Derek and his wife Ellen roared with laughter.

'That's got to be Doris,' said Ellen. 'That's just what she would say.'

In the space of a few short years, ever since Derek first interviewed Doris for TV-am, the Jamesons had become close friends. They visited her often, spoke frequently on the phone and when she was lying in hospital, Derek and Ellen were amongst her last visitors.

They don't regard the friendship as over just because Doris passed away last year. They are convinced she is still nearby, taking a keen interest in their affairs.

'These old ladies keep writing to me to say they've seen Doris,' said Derek. 'One insisted that she saw Doris' face close to mine on the TV screen. Others write with messages from Doris. One lady recently said that Doris told her to tell me to take it easy. "He's doing too much," she said. "He needs to rest and relax more."

'Which is exactly what Ellen says too! But I'm sure Doris is around somewhere helping me. The strangest things have happened.

'I was writing my autobiography recently and it was difficult because I didn't have any pictures of me as a child and publishers always want a few pictures in autobiographies. The trouble was, in those days we were so poor, people didn't have cameras. I didn't make any public appeals for help, yet suddenly, in the space of five or six weeks, five people who knew me as a child or knew the neighbourhood where I was brought up, spontaneously got in touch and three sent pictures of me as a boy – one of them came from New Zealand.

'They all said things like, "I've seen you on television over the years and thought that one day I'd contact you. Now I am. Do you recognize this picture?"

'There was nothing for fifty years and then suddenly they all turned up in a matter of weeks. I said to Ellen, "That's Doris, I reckon." '

Then there was the matter of the book's title.

'I planned to write a book about Fleet Street called *Who's Got the Mother?'* said Derek. 'In newspapers when there's a big story, someone's bought up the wife, someone else has the neighbour and you're an editor left with nothing and you say belligerently at conference, "Who's got the mother?"

'So that was the perfect title for a sort of *Hot Metal*-type book on Fleet Street. Anyway the publishers came along and asked for a synopsis.

'I put some paper in the typewriter. I hadn't the faintest idea what I was going to write. I put down, "Working Title: . . ." and then, without a second's hesitation, I added, "Touched by Angels".

'I'd never thought of that title. It hadn't been in my mind in any shape or form. It just came out quite spontaneously. I'm sure it was Doris nudging me because it was absolutely right.

'I grew up in a home for waifs and strays in the East End in the 1930s. I was illegitimate. I didn't even know my mother at that time, and I never met my father. The old girl who brought me up was Mrs Wren (Agnes Wren), known by us as Ma Wren.

'She raised over seventy kids. Some of them were dumped on her doorstep and she never got a penny from the state. She did it all on her own. Some of the girls with illegitimate babies might pay her five shillings a week for a while, then disappear. Others came and took their babies back. Yet Ma got on with it as best she could.

'We lived in total poverty and sometimes if I was down in the dumps she used to touch the dimple on my chin and say, "You'll be all right. You're touched by angels!"

'And perhaps she was right, because all my life I've had the feeling that some force I don't understand has directed me. I've never had much control over the course of my life; it's all just happened. So when I suddenly got that title I felt I was getting a bit of help from upstairs.

'Ma Wren was psychic. She used to read the tea leaves. There was a tatty old bit of curtain that hung at the bottom of the dresser and I would sit behind the curtain with all the old boots and shoes and rubbish and listen to Ma carrying on over the tea leaves.

'At the age of seven I discovered that the housewives in the neighbourhood who gave her tuppence didn't have such a rosy future as those who gave her a tanner!

'Ma Wren never bothered to read my tea leaves – I was just a kid – but she did give me the reassurance that I would be okay in life. Somehow she got that over very forcibly.

'Ma Wren used to swear as well, every few seconds, and then she'd say, "God forgive me for swearing. You little swine."

' "What's for dinner, Ma?" we used to ask.

' "Shit with sugar on. God forgive me for swearing," she'd reply.

'But she was a big, cuddly, comforting woman and Doris was the nearest thing on earth to Ma Wren that I've ever met. She was the same type. A lovely, warm, expansive, grandmotherly figure. I used to say she was my adopted grandmother.

'I met Doris for the first time at TV-am. Doris was living in her flat in Fulham then and she was booked to appear about eight. Apparently, early that morning she and John had the telly on to watch the first part of the show and she saw me.

' "Oh no," she said to John, "I didn't know that Derek Jameson was going to be on. He'll tear me to shreds."

'She was thinking, rough, tough newspaper editor. Then the car arrived to take her to the studio and she was travelling along thinking that I was going to make her look a fool. Then she arrived in the Green Room and I said, "Hello, Doris, love. I've been wanting to meet you for a long time," and she was so taken aback.

'It turned out that we had a great natural affinity. Like me, Doris had come from total poverty. Not just poor, but grinding poverty. She had risen above it, got on and become a household name loved by millions of people – and I suppose you could say the same thing happened to me!

'What's more, there was a great deal of psychic influence in my life. Everyone tells me I'm psychic and that I've got healing powers and so on. I've never developed it but I've been fascinated by psychic phenomena all my life. I'm a powerful supporter of spiritualism and alternative medicine. I realise that there's another dimension out there and there are things we know nothing about. My great ambition in life has always been to tap the source and find out more about the truth of the life beyond. I'm quite convinced there *is* a life beyond and I'm quite convinced that spiritualism is a true and genuine force for good.

'I've had psychic experiences of my own. In moments of emotion I always know who's on the phone before I pick it up, and I knew when Pat, my foster sister from the home, died.

'We were brought up together and in later life I saw Pat once every year or two. Anyway, I heard that she was seriously ill so I went to see her. I didn't have any knowledge of the circumstances but when I went to see her I realized she had cancer. Then one Monday afternoon I was off-duty (I was editor of the *News of the World* at the time and we had Monday's off) and about two in the afternoon I was hit by the most terrible pains I have ever experienced in my life. My whole body was being torn apart as if people were sticking swords into me. I was on the bed writhing in agony for about two hours.

'Then just as suddenly as it had begun, the pain lifted and an hour later the phone rang.

' "That'll be to say that Pat's died," I said to Ellen.

'Sure enough it was her son to say she'd died that afternoon. Yet before those pains I didn't even know she was close to death.

'Although we hadn't seen a lot of each other over the years I think there was a tremendous bond between us, forged when we were both fighting for survival. We were the bottom of the heap, often not knowing where our next meal was coming from. We weren't just living,

73

we were fighting for survival and that created a great spiritual affinity between us. I'm sure that's why I felt Pat's death pangs.

'Many times I've been asked why I stand up for Doris, why I'm a friend of hers and why I support her. Well, I always say that whether you believe in spiritualism or not, it doesn't matter. What you can't do is deny the great comfort, joy, warmth and support Doris brought to thousands of people around the world, and for that alone she ought to be revered and remembered with respect and love.

'And she is by the general public. Not the clever, clever newspapermen and the feature writers who were out to trip her up. Not the scoffers and the sceptics, but the ordinary man and woman in the street have always loved Doris and I know why. Because she was warm and loving and caring.

'Of course, in the end she was hassled and it all got too much for her. She always fought back robustly against her critics and that endeared her to me, but underneath she was deeply hurt by it all. One cross word in a newspaper would upset her for days. She'd phone up all her friends and come on the phone to Ellen and me because, naturally, being a Fleet Street editor I could give her some words of comfort.

'When she was close to the end she said to me, "Enjoy every minute of it, Derek. It's getting bigger all the time. Don't let them get you down. You're going to have to grow another skin. I've never managed it but that's what you need to do. You deserve all that's coming to you. We've both worked bloody hard all our lives and we deserve a bit of comfort in our old age."

'The saddest thing of all was when I went to see her at the hospital the day before the operation. She clung to my hand and she was so upset. I think she feared the worst and sensed she was coming to the end.

' "Derek, it's not that I'm afraid of passing over. I know that can only bring joy and happiness. But what's so upsetting is that I haven't done half the things I wanted to do. It's only in the last year or two I've been able to enjoy the good things in life and now it's all being taken away."

'So she knew she was going. It wasn't that she was afraid but that she hadn't been able to fulfil herself now that she'd reached the situation when for the first time in her life she had money.

'For years and years she told me she used to trek all over the country on buses and trains at 10.30 or 11.00 at night, waiting for a bus in the pouring rain, in return for a fee of ten shillings and sixpence plus her fares. That was the life she led for all those years and now she'd made the big time and was a world famous celebrity but her body packed up on her.

'It was a great shame because she was a wonderful woman.

'I miss her desperately. Especially if things are getting a bit complicated and heavy and I don't know which way to turn. It would be nice to phone Doris and see what she's got to say. But I don't feel she's far away. I'm sure she's close by, giving me a helping hand.'

ELLEN JAMESON

Derek Jameson never did have a sitting with Doris. She volunteered many times but Derek always refused. He needed no proof, and since his family background was so tangled he was sure he wouldn't know half the people Doris might mention.

It would be far better, he felt, if she saved her energy for people who needed it more. His journalist wife Ellen, however, was the surprised recipient of a spontaneous message.

'We'd gone to see Doris at her old flat in Fulham and there was a terrible noise going on. They were doing building work outside,' said Ellen.

' "I was going to give you a sitting this afternoon," Doris said, "but I can't with all that noise going on."

'We told her it didn't matter at all but then suddenly she said, "Hang on. Was your mother's name Amy?"

'Mamie,' I told her.

' "Oh well, I think she's here," said Doris, and she started chatting away.

'Then she said, "Your dad was in the RAF, wasn't he?"

'I said yes.

' "What rank was he?" she asked.

'I was just about to answer, when she said, "No, I'm not asking you. I'm asking your mum." Then she started laughing and said, "Your mum's quite a character. She said, 'Well you, Doris, would have had to call him Chiefie!' "

'I didn't know whether that was right but I found out later that, apparently, with Doris' rank in the RAF and my dad's rank in the RAF she would have had to call him Chiefie.

'She came up with my family's names. She talked about my ex-husband and where he worked. Things like that.

'When we got home and Derek and I talked it all through, we said that either she's got a hotline to upstairs or she's spent a fortune having me tailed and checked out, which was highly unlikely.

'I was very happy about this. I'd tried several times to get in touch with my mum and I was always looking for something definite but I'd never got it before. I think that's one of the problems with a lot of mediums. It's very easy to say, "I've got your mother here." Then if you say, "My mother's still alive, they reply "It's your grandmother then." With Doris there was always something extra – those few little details that were absolutely right which gave you something positive to hang on to.

'She freed me. After that I didn't need anything else. It closed a chapter of my life. I knew that my mother was all right, she was around and looked after me and cared for me, and knowing that, I could get on with my life without looking back. Although I spent a lot of time with Doris after that I never had another sitting.

'Funnily enough, when I first met her she leaned across the table and said, "You read the tarot cards, don't you?"

'I wasn't sure what her views on this were but I said yes, not knowing what I was letting myself in for. I expected a lecture or something but instead she said, "You could be a good medium, you know. I'll have you on the platform working within a year!"

'The strange thing was that she did. Only I wasn't working as a medium. She had me on stage chairing her meetings for her!

'I remember once at the theatre in Newcastle she asked me to go to the manager and pick up the mail. Letters were handed in at the theatre where she appeared and she never opened them till after the meeting. So that particular night I collected the mail and took it, unopened, back to the hotel with me.

77

'The next morning, Doris said, "Would you go through them and sort them into piles – this one for answering, this one for an appointment, or whatever?"

'Well, I did that for a couple of hours, then I went and sat down beside her on the settee and said, "This job must break your heart sometimes, Doris. Some of these letters . . ."

'Well, they were almost too tragic to read.

' "Oh, you're talking about the little black girl," said Doris.

' "Yes," I said in surprise. Doris hadn't seen any of the letters yet she knew which story had upset me most.

' "Yes, she's sitting beside you. She's got those little beads in her hair and I'd say she was about seven."

' "You've got it wrong, Doris," I teased. "She was eight two days before she died."

'The little girl had been murdered by her father. He was actually in prison for her murder and the letter, which I opened along with dozens of others and which had not been near Doris at all, was written by the mother. She wanted to know if there was any chance of seeing Doris.

'I looked at the envelope. It was a local letter which had been handed in at the theatre.

'Doris asked me to phone the mother and tell her to come to the theatre that night. But before I could get to the phone she stopped me.

' "No, don't," she said, "because if I get a message for her and anyone finds out that you phoned and asked her to come, they'd say it was set up or something."

'It was such a shame, but once again I was impressed. Out of the huge pile of letters which she hadn't seen or touched she'd picked up this terrible tragedy and knew all about it. I never needed any more evidence from her.

'I went on tour with Doris a couple of times and she never rested. She was doing sittings all the time. Every time room service delivered a cup of tea Doris would give them a message. They used to queue up at the door to bring her things so that they might get a message.

'Doris did for other people what she did for me. She gave them back their lives to live. People could say there's no point in mourning, he's there, he can see me, he's OK, and now I can go forward and get on with the rest of my life.'

TONI ARTHUR

Like Derek Jameson, television personality Toni Arthur met Doris at TV-am. Doris felt it was important to spread her message as widely as possible and she rarely refused an interview.

So, early one morning she set off for the TV-am studios at Camden Lock to talk to presenter Toni Arthur.

'Doris was a lovely lady,' said Toni. 'I remember she came into the studio and gave me a cuddle. Not a "hello darling" kiss on the cheek and then off. A real, warm cuddle.

'We were chatting in the Green Room before I went on when she suddenly told me that my grandmother was watching over me. My grandmother's name, she said, was Harriet.

'Well, I wasn't sure about this but it was time to go on. Doris waited in the wings while I went out to interview the lady from Battersea Dogs Home who was appearing immediately before Doris.

'It was very funny. The woman had brought several dogs with her and they were jumping about all over the place while we talked about finding a home for stray dogs.

' "Sit down!" the lady kept saying to one dog that was jumping up and down all over me, but it took no notice at all.

'Anyway, like a good interviewer I ploughed on as if nothing was happening but unknown to me one of the dogs poohed on the floor. Well, I hadn't noticed it and I was carrying on, talking to the camera and walking this way and that, completely unaware that I was about to put my foot in it, quite literally!

'Doris told me afterwards that she'd seen the whole thing.

' "Your grandmother was laughing like a drain," she said, "and we were both willing you as hard as we could not to walk in it."

'She must have realized that if I did I wouldn't have been able to change my shoes for two and a half hours.

'Well, I looked at the tape afterwards and it was extraordinary. How I didn't tread in that pile, I'll never know. I walked over it and round it and across it – each time it looks as if I'm about to step in it and then somehow I miss it. At one point I was standing practically on it but it was between my high heel and the sole – missing my shoe altogether.

'It's only a tiny thing, of course, but it really was amazing. I'm sure I must have been getting outside help.

'Afterwards, Doris came on and did the interview, and later she went back to the subject of my grandmother. She'd got it wrong, she said, apparently the name she'd given me was that of my grandmother's sister and it was her middle name. She was called Phyllis Harriet.

'Well, to be honest, I didn't even know my grand-mother had a sister let alone what her name might have been, but I checked with my father afterwards and it turned out she was absolutely right.

'Doris' effect on the studio was extraordinary. Cam-eramen are cynical types but they were fascinated. There were people hanging around where they don't normally do so, all to get a glimpse of her. Nobody would admit it, of course. They tried to find reasons for being there but it was too much of a coincidence. As for the other guests in the Green Room, they were spell-bound.

'I only met Doris once, I'm sorry to say, but since then I've talked to a lot of people and I know that she gave an awful lot of comfort. Whether you believe or don't believe, you can't deny that.

'We're in such a state today. There are so few people to trust. Nobody trusts doctors or politicians, few people go to church, so anyone who can give succour is greatly needed. The critics who knock Doris don't do anyone any favours.

'Doris was never a bad woman. She gave help and love and happiness.

'It amazes me how mediums are treated. Nobody would think of saying to an artist, sit down and paint a picture now, but they expect a medium to turn the tap on immediately and if it doesn't always work, they crit-icize. Well, I would ask the critics if they've ever had an off-day.

'I couldn't disbelieve Doris and I think people like her make life worth living for other people.'

Doris fixed Rusty Lee with her penetrating blue eyes.

'Now, Rusty,' she said, 'Your father wants you to know that you mustn't worry. He knows you're upset but everything'll be fine.'

Rusty Lee, cook, actress and TV personality was stunned.

'I'd been having some worries. I was going through a very hard time,' she said, 'but Doris knew nothing about it. I hadn't discussed it with her. I don't think she even knew I'd lost my father, so I was amazed when she suddenly came out with that. It gave me a lot of comfort.

'We first met at London Weekend Television when we were waiting to go into the studio for *An Audience with Edna Everage*. We'd all been invited along as guests. That was before I got *Game For a Laugh* . . .

'Anyway, I was with my husband, David, and Doris was with John and we got talking. I thought she was lovely. A friendly housewife with no airs and graces. She was just naturally a darling.

'It breaks my heart when people say nasty things about her. I know she wasn't the sort of person to do anything wrong. And I'm very glad I got the chance to know her because she wasn't like other people.

'We became friends and I used to ring her when I was going to be in London and she would ring me when she was going to be in Birmingham. She invited me to the Birmingham Odeon to see her show once and it was just totally breathtaking. David and I sat in the audience and I think you could have heard a pin drop. Nobody wanted to miss a word she said. The atmosphere was wonderful and outside everyone had been queuing up to see her for hours. David and I had never seen anything like it.

'It was funny because beforehand David thought it was all a load of rubbish but at the end of the evening he was stunned. He said you just can't explain it. It gave you goose pimples all over.

'I remember her saying to a couple that their little baby had passed away. She called them up from the balcony and she told them the baby's name. She said he was holding something small in his hands which they'd buried him with but she couldn't see what it was. They told her it was a toy frog. It was one of his favourite toys and they'd put it in the coffin with him.

'Everyone was in tears yet we all wanted more. She must have been on stage for two hours yet you wanted more at the end. You didn't want her to go. The relief she gave people! A lot of people had doubts to start with but afterwards they were amazed. Doris gave names, pet names and all kinds of details she couldn't possibly have known. The ones who got messages were so totally relieved.

'I was glad my husband was there to see it because it was a wonderful experience. There was nothing bad or unhealthy or harmful about it.

'After that, Doris invited me to sit on the stage with her at another show. Well, I was very nervous. I stood there shaking while she introduced me to the audience but they were wonderful to me. I had to read something out, I think. I enjoyed it very much.

'All these terrible things they are saying now about her cheating – it's so wrong. I was with her that whole evening and I saw nothing underhand at all.

'She wasn't reading up on anything or talking to people. They were queuing up outside. They wanted to give her flowers and letters but she said, "Oh Rusty,

I daren't let them come in or people will say I'm getting information from them."

'So we sat there in the dressing-room, eating sandwiches and cake and drinking tea. The only time she left the room was to go to the loo. I saw nothing untoward at all. When we were on stage she was getting contacts all over the place. There were people who didn't want to come out when she mentioned their details, so she'd say, "All right, I know you are in this area here."

'One woman this happened to did come out in the end. She was a shy, nervous girl but she was pleased with her message and relieved to have got it.

'I remember one woman she talked to was heart-broken because her husband had gone out to work one day and not come back. Well, Doris told her what had happened. Apparently he had been knocked down at the side of the road as he was crossing over.

' "He was right beside the kerb and there was a bank on the corner," said Doris. And it was right.

'The husband wanted his wife to know how much he loved her. Well, that woman was so thrilled. I'm sure it made her day. It was a wonderful evening.

'Even though we lived a long way apart we spoke often on the phone. Doris had a marvellous sense of humour and we'd yak yak yak for ages. She was so pleased when she moved into her house and she told me all about it. I heard all about the pictures of the spirit children too.

'Last April I had to go into hospital for a hysterectomy and Doris phoned to cheer me up.

' "I had to laugh," she said. "You were in hospital and you were still getting out press releases!"

' "Well, you have to keep working," I told her.

'She didn't seem ill herself though she must have been because it wasn't long after that that she died. It was so sudden. I was shocked and dreadfully upset.

'I will always love her. I think of her often even today and I feel her close to me – particularly when I'm going through a bad patch. I can almost hear her saying in that lovely voice, "Don't worry, love. It'll be all right."

'I'd love her to have seen my new show and the musical I did. The critics thought I was going to be terrible but when it came out they said they were surprised and gave me nice reviews. I would like Doris to have been there to see it. But then perhaps she was.

'I'll always miss her but I really feel she's not far away.'

DORIS COLLINS

Before her last illness, Doris Stokes frequently spoke to her colleague Doris Collins on the telephone.

'The papers tried to make us out to be bitter enemies and rivals,' said top medium Doris Collins, 'but that wasn't true at all. It was just paper talk to sell papers. In fact we often spoke about three times a week.

'We both toured the country giving demonstrations, we both wrote books and had to do book publicity, we both had to deal with bereaved people every day. We understood each other's problems.'

So if Doris Stokes was going to come back from the spirit world to have a chat, the person she was likely to turn to was Doris Collins.

Since Doris Stokes passed away in 1987 many mediums have claimed to have heard from her but Doris Collins believes most of such claims to be wishful thinking.

'Some time ago, Doris came back to me,' she said 'She only came the once, but at that time I'm sure I was the only one she'd spoken to.

'She was very concerned because, apparently, some medium had come out with a message that Doris had hidden some money in Jersey which could not be found.

'Anyway, that particular day I hadn't even been thinking about her when suddenly she was there.

' "I haven't spoken to anyone, Doris, you know that," she said. "Tell them to stop it. Tell them to stop looking for something I haven't got. I've got no money in Jersey."

'She seemed very concerned that there was a lot of fuss and trouble being stirred up about nothing.

'Well, I can believe her. I'm sure Doris didn't have any money in Jersey. She wasn't an educated person and she didn't know the first thing about getting money out of the country. It wouldn't have crossed her mind.

'We first met just after Doris came to London. She and John came to see me work at Balham – it's quite usual for one medium to go and watch another – and afterwards I gave them a lift home because they didn't have a car.

'Doris wasn't well-known then. She'd just started working at SAGB, but she was sincere and dedicated to her work and totally committed.

'I never did see her work because once things started moving for her we were both working at the same time. We were even in Australia at the same time although miles apart geographically.

'In some ways it's probably good that I didn't ever see her because the papers that were trying to promote this enemy idea were always asking me to make some sort of comment about her work, probably in the hope that they could twist it. Fortunately, I was able to answer quite truthfully that they couldn't expect me to pass an opinion on work I've never seen.

'In fact, Doris was a good medium who opened a door through her work to allow many psychics to become popular. She was a totally honest person. She was very flattered that she had reached such a pinnacle in her life, and why not? She deserved it.

'I think the only pity is that it all came too quickly. Had it happened more gradually she would have been better able to cope.

'The other unfortunate thing is that Doris couldn't get away from her work. She didn't have any hobbies as far as I know and I think it's an important safety valve to have other interests because a medium's work is very draining emotionally.

'Personally I do a lot of petit point and I like to keep my garden going. You need something like that to relax you.

'You have to accept that there are going to be difficulties, scandals and jealousy and that the press are going to try to pull you down and destroy you because that sells newspapers. It's not fair, but then life isn't fair. You just have to get on with it.

'Mediums also have to put up with all these magicians saying they can do what we do. Let them stand up there for two and a half hours without any props and do it, that's what I always say. They've never attempted it yet.

'It's not an easy life being a medium but once you're a medium you can't give it up. It's not just a job. Like Doris Stokes, I don't think I'll ever retire.'

Guitarist

Bert Weedon first met Doris Stokes in Danny La Rue's dressing-room.

'Danny was an old friend and he'd invited me to the Prince of Wales Theatre to see his show, *Hello Dolly*,' said Bert. 'Afterwards we were backstage, walking to his dressing-room, when he said, "I've got a lady here who's dying to meet you," and we went in and he introduced me to the lady who was sitting there.

' "This is Doris Stokes," he said.

'Well I knew the name of course. I'd read about Doris in the papers.

' "Your name's well known to me, Doris," I told her.

'She was very easy to get on with. We started talking and Doris mentioned that she'd been trying to get a record of mine, without success.

' "*Bert Weedon Remembers Jim Reeves*," she said, "but I just can't find it anywhere."

' "I'm afraid it's a very old record and it's been deleted, Doris," I explained.

'But as it happened I had a few copies at home and I sent her one. Our friendship just grew from there and I knew Doris about six or seven years, I think.

'As I got to know her, she told me she was making a record and she asked my advice about various things because she knew I'd made hundreds of records while for her it was a completely new venture.

' "You wouldn't play on my record, Bert, would you?" she asked one day.

' "Of course I would, love," I said. "What's it called?"

' "Well, I thought I'd call it, *Welcome to My World*," she said.

' "OK," I said, "Why don't I play an opening theme called 'Welcome to My World' and you can talk over that."

'Doris liked the idea so I wrote some music for her. Then a bit later she mentioned that she'd got a poem she'd like to use.

' "I don't suppose you could set that to music, could you?" she asked.

' "Certainly," I said.'

The poem was called 'In a Baby Castle', a favourite of Doris'. She heard it spoken to her when she was grieving for her baby son who had died tragically at five months old. Doris never forgot the words which had given her so much comfort and she wanted to include them on her record.

'I wrote a little tune and Doris was thrilled to bits with it,' said Bert.

'Soon after that she was doing a big show at the Dominion Theatre in Tottenham Court Road and she asked me to go along and appear with her.

'It was a fascinating experience. I saw at first hand how tremendously helpful she was to thousands of people. She gave the audience such an uplift. It was marvellous to see the people's faces after the demonstration. She gave such comfort to people whose lives had been upturned by losing their dear ones. Love simply poured out of her and she had a lovely sense of humour, too.

'A lot of show-business people knew and liked her because she was a real trooper. She would go on tour working long hours in difficult circumstances, even when she was ill. She hated the thought of cancelling a demonstration and disappointing people. Yet through it all she retained a sense of humour.

'She was such a lovely person that you just wanted to help her in any way you could. I remember I was able to give her a few hints about appearing on stage. There's a way of walking on stage and walking off. A way of sitting. A way of arranging the lights. Not in order to make it theatrical but just to make it as pleasant as possible for the audience.

'Doris was always very grateful for anything you could do for her.

'When I first knew her she was living in a little flat in Fulham and one evening when my wife Maggie and I were visiting she got Dick Emery to come through. He was an old friend of mine and he gave me a message through Doris that only I could understand.

'There was no way Doris could have known about it.

'Some time after that the BBC wanted to make a programme about Doris called *40 Minutes*. Doris was still in her flat and she was a bit worried because it was so small it wasn't really suitable for a film crew and all the paraphernalia.

' "Bert," she said one day on the phone, "D'you think we could make the film at your house?"

'She'd been to visit Maggie and me at home in Buckinghamshire and she loved the house and all the space. We've got a two-acre garden and a swimming pool and she loved to sit by that.

' "Of course you can, love," I told her.

'So they all came down and we sat in the garden and straight away Doris struck up a rapport with the crew. She made them all laugh and every now and then she would give a little message to someone, which astounded them.

'Maggie, who is a marvellous cook, made some of the cakes Doris loved and it was a very happy time.

'We saw Doris in less happy circumstances, too, yet she never changed. I remember once when she was very ill in hospital we visited her. Despite the fact that she must have been feeling dreadful she was cheerful and friendly and you could see that everyone loved her. Some patients get grouchy and hospital staff have a hard time liking them but here the nurses and doctors loved Doris.

'As for Doris and Maggie, they got on like a house on fire. Maggie is very psychic. She is very good at psychometry. In fact Doris told her that if she developed her gifts she could be a medium. so they had a lot in common but they also got on well as women.

'Doris admired the way Maggie had decorated the house and when she bought a place of her own she asked for some tips.

' "I love the way you've done your curtains," she'd say, "I think I'll copy that, Maggie. Do you mind?"

' "Of course I don't mind," Maggie would reply, "but why don't you try this and this . . ."

'And she'd make all sorts of suggestions to help Doris make the best of the individual features of her own home.

'Knowing Doris made me realize all over again that great people in all walks of life are usually humble. You don't have to be bombastic when you've got a great gift. You are what you are and that's all that counts.'

Bert Weedon has always been interested in spiritualism, yet he says that far from being gullible this interest has made him more sceptical than most about people who claim psychic powers.

'Ever since I was a child I've had an interest in philosophy and religion,' he explained. 'I read lots of books on different religions and philosophies and it seemed to me that this small world of ours can't be the only thing in existence. There has to be something after life.

'As young as fourteen I attended some meetings and demonstrations of spiritualism but I never took anything at face value. I would never accept everything I was told. I always weigh things up and judge them for myself.

'I've seen a lot of people who imagine they are mediums and they are not. They are deluding themselves. I've also seen people who are supposed to be good mediums and they've been awful. So I'm not wide-eyed. I view such claims with scepticism until the person proves that what they say is true.

'There was no doubt, of course, about Doris. She was a simple, loving person. She gave so much love to this world. I'm sure the world is a better place because she was here.'

FAY HILLIER

John Inman was coming to tea.

The word swept round the holiday park where Doris had her seaside retreat and by mid-afternoon a great many residents just happened to be at home and just happened to be stationed not far from their windows so that if an unfamiliar car went by they couldn't help but notice the occupants.

Over in the Stokes' cottage John and Doris were fussing around; Doris in high excitement, John wondering whether all the effort was worth while.

Doris was particularly pleased because the daughter of one of her Sheppey friends was a caterer and she had promised to lay on a special tea for the celebrities.

It was all ready far too soon, of course, but at last, just after four o'clock, the guests arrived and Doris sat back to enjoy an entertaining afternoon.

'We had a wonderful time,' she said afterwards, 'and we were sorry to see them go when they had to leave at eight.'

There was a special word of thanks for actress Fay Hillier because Fay, who was appearing in a show with John Inman, had arranged the whole thing.

'We met when a mutual friend took me along to meet Doris at her house,' said Fay.

Fay, who had been the girl-friend of the late Dick Emery, had never met a medium before.

'I was quite sceptical. I was still grieving for Dick at the time but I certainly wasn't expecting to talk about it,' she said. 'I went simply out of interest because this friend had invited me.

'What struck me first was Doris' amazing warmth. She was very much an earth-mother figure. So much love came out of her.

'Anyway we had a cup of tea and Doris started telling me all these things about Dick. Everything she said was true and I found it very comforting. She knew I was still clinging on. I hadn't been able to let go and the things she said helped me to do so. Which I needed. I had to get on with life.

'I was truly amazed and quite shaky. I cried with amazement.

'After that I was so intrigued I went to see one of her meetings in the theatre. The thing about Doris was that whether you believed in her or not, she did not seem to do anything other than comfort people. She didn't promise the earth or make tons of money or push herself on people.

93

'It was a very moving evening. I was standing in the wings and at one point I had to rush off and walk up and down the corridor crying. I couldn't control myself and that was unusual for me because as an actress you are used to controlling your feelings. There had been a baby killed and Doris felt the pain in the place where the baby was hurt. She suddenly grabbed her chest. It was all true and everybody backstage was howling. It was so touching and correct.

'It was emotional and the parents had a good cry but it was a release for them. A healthy thing, as I knew from my own experience. It doesn't do any good to keep the grief locked up inside you.

'Doris and I became good friends. I often went to the theatre with her and soon she had me giving out the flowers for her at the end of the evening. Then one night the person who normally chaired the meetings couldn't come so she asked me to take over. I thought it was a great honour and this time I managed to get through the evening without crying though I did have to swallow hard a couple of times.

'We were often in touch. I was always surprised and pleased that she phoned me when she wanted a friendly ear to pour out her own troubles to. And she always seemed to know when I was feeling low.

'Sometimes I'd be weeping in cupboards and not telling anyone and then out of the blue the phone would ring and it would be Doris.

' "I know you're feeling unhappy so I thought I'd give you a ring," she'd say.

'Her powers were astonishing. I took a lot of theatre friends to see her and everybody found it amazing. Nobody left indifferent. John Inman was astounded.

'She would often come out with tiny little pieces of information that were quite correct just like other people would remark on the weather. She knew when I'd moved a photograph or put something away that used to stand out on display. Only little things but always absolutely right. I remember she even forecast my son's wedding before I had any idea he was even thinking of getting married.

'He was only twenty. Then one day towards the end of the year, Doris said there would be a big family reunion the following April. It would be a big do and the whole family would be there.

'I've got one of those enormous families which is spread all over the place so it's extremely rare for all of us to get together.

' "Well, that would be nice," I said, "but I can't imagine what it would be for."

'The next month my son announced, out of the blue, that he wanted to get married in April.

'We had that big reunion just as Doris had predicted.

'It was a nice warm friendship between us, and now she's gone I miss her a lot. It's horrid not having her there to talk to.

'But she changed my life. She opened my eyes to be able to accept spiritualism as something healthy. She also restored my faith in human nature. It was such a change to find someone who cares when you come up against so many people who don't care at all.'

The Media

FRANK DURHAM

Frank Durham didn't recognize his grandfather at first.

'I've got a William here,' said Doris. 'Do you know a William?'

Frank's mind went blank.

'I can't think of one at the moment,' he said.

'Never mind, I'll ask him something else,' said Doris.

There was a brief pause.

'That William goes with Emma.'

That was when it clicked.

'William was my grandfather's name and Emma was my grandmother,' recalled Frank. 'It seemed pretty clear that Doris had got my grandfather so I waited eagerly to hear what earth-shattering message he was bringing from the other side.

' "Your grandfather says," Doris went on, "to tell you that the beer here is free."

'That was it! It wouldn't exactly change the course of human history but since Grandad was a well-known beer connoisseur it seemed a reasonable message from one connoisseur to another!'

Frank Durham was the first national newspaper journalist outside spiritualist circles to interview Doris. He had just started his own feature agency and he was always on the look-out for interesting or quirky subjects that he could turn into features to sell to the world's press.

Psychic stories were always popular and Frank regularly checked the columns of *Psychic News* for new names which might interest a wider public.

'One day I saw a little piece about this medium who had just come down from the North of England,' said Frank. 'Her name was Doris Stokes and she sounded as if she might be interesting so I went to see her.

'She was living in straightened circumstances in this awful grey block of flats in Fulham. I remember it was a Saturday afternoon and Chelsea had been playing at home and there were all these yobs and hooligans in the street.

'The flats were all the same but outside Doris' front door she'd decorated the balcony with pots of flowers and there were lots of little touches to make it a bit different.

'Doris was a very warm, unpretentious person and absolutely elated about being interviewed. She loved being in the paper.

'We had a nice cup of tea and got on with the interview. It was only afterwards that she came out with this stuff about my grandfather.

'Actually, it was my father who came through first. She suddenly started talking to someone who seemed to be standing behind my right shoulder.

' "It's your father," she told me, "but he will only say that he's Mr Durham and he won't talk to me because he doesn't agree with this sort of thing!"

'Fortunately, my grandfather was more cooperative. Actually, even more impressive was the bit that came next. My grandfather didn't have anything terribly significant to say but after a while Doris got someone else.

' "I've got somebody here for you," she said, "but I can't understand what he's saying. It's some strange thing like, 'Don't let the bastards grind you down. Pictures are worth a thousand words.' I don't know what he's talking about. He's rambling on like that. All I can make out is he died in the bath. He seems a bit embarrassed about that. 'Don't worry about it, love. People have died in more embarrassing situations than that!' "

'This was very impressive because the picture editor of one of the magazines I worked for did die in the bath and he was always drunk and always saying these strange things about pictures being worth a thousand words. He spoke like that the whole time.

' "Don't worry about him not making sense," I told Doris. 'He didn't make sense when he was alive.'

'I must admit I was impressed. I'd gone along there, seeing Doris as nothing more than a story. But she seemed incredible. She even told me I would go and work in America which I didn't believe at the time. I thought she was getting mixed up because I'd already been to South America, but in fact she was right. I've worked part of the year in America ever since.'

Frank was pleased but not as surprised by his encounter with Doris as some people might have been. His research into psychic stories for purely commercial reasons had led him to meet a number of remarkable people.

'Psychic stories are popular,' said Frank, 'but you have to check them out. Anybody can say anything. I always want proof before I write my story. I remember I wrote a feature for *Woman's Own* about a couple who claimed to conduct psychic operations. The woman was an office cleaner, her husband a motor mechanic. They claimed to have cured a Maltese girl living in Britain who was dying of cancer of the cervix. Not only had they cured her, they said, but she was now married and pregnant.

98

'Well, of course, anyone can make up a story like that, so I checked. The girl had gone back to live in Malta but as luck would have it she returned to Britain to visit relatives and she was able to talk to me. She was indeed pregnant, yet she'd been so ill with cancer that she had to carry a card in her handbag so that if the pain got too bad she could walk into any hospital casualty department and get pain-killing shots.

'I asked her for the name of the doctor who treated her and I rang him.

' "Did you treat this lady for an inoperable tumour?" I asked.

He confirmed that he did and that she was a terminal case.

' "Well, she now has no sign of any tumour. In fact she's pregnant," I told him.

'There was a long silence and at last he said very guardedly, "Path labs can make mistakes, you know."

'As far as I was concerned, that story held up.

'Around this time I wrote another similar story for *Woman's Own* about a school for Psychic Healers in Blackheath. I went down and interviewed the principal of the school. He couldn't give me any personal proof of what he claimed so I asked him to give me a list of patients he had cured. He agreed and I contacted them. Several were civil servants and people with quite lofty positions but they were so grateful for the help this man had given them that they were prepared to overcome their embarrassment and speak out about their cures.

'Once again I felt I had proof that the story was true, so I used it and it appeared in the magazine.'

Frank felt so much at ease with Doris after his interview with her that he saw her quite frequently after that.

'I often called in for a cup of tea and a chat when I was near her flat in Fulham, 'he said. 'At the time she was conducting an evening class for trainee mediums – known as a developing circle to spiritualists – and I asked if I could go along to one.

'The class was held in a room at Fulham Town Hall. I remember it was a large room with a big horseshoe-shaped table in the middle. These kids sat around the table and tried to pick up things from the spirit world. I was to be their exercise for the night.

' "Now what can you tell me about our guest tonight?" Doris asked the kids and she went round from one to the other collecting their impressions. They didn't know me from Adam and most of them got nothing at all. They said the sort of things that mediums tend to say when they're marking time.

'Then suddenly Doris got to one girl and she said, "His name is Wilhelm, Franz Wilhelm and all I can see is a field of poppies."

'This was extraordinary because although Doris knew my name was Frank she had no idea that my second name is William or that I'd just come back from Flanders, famous, of course, for its poppy fields. Even if she'd wanted to. Doris couldn't have primed them with that information.'

Frank wrote about the psychic evening classes afterwards and some months later he turned to Doris again.

'I met a man who was worried that his house was haunted,' said Frank. 'I think the place had an unpleasant atmosphere and there were probably unexplained knocks and bangs. Anyway he was quite sure there was something there so I took Doris down to see if there was anything she could do.

'It seemed to be a perfectly normal house near Sevenoaks in Kent. It was detached with a bit of ground

round it and it was quite old. There were a few oak beams about, although how old it was I wouldn't like to guess.

'Anyway, Doris walked round the house and she stopped dead in one particular place where she said there was a cold spot which was the source of the trouble. It turned out that this was the exact spot where a previous tenant had hanged himself.

'Doris tuned in and had a chat with this person. I don't think she could exorcize spirits as such, she just tried to persuade them to go away and stop bothering the people in the house.

'Whether it worked or not, I've no idea, but the man who called us down seemed very happy with it all.

'I kept in contact with Doris while she lived in Fulham. She even invited me to the *Psychic News* knees-up – an annual dinner-dance. She knew I didn't believe just anything I was told and she liked that. Even when she became famous she liked to talk to me on an ordinary level. But later, when she moved away, we lost touch. I didn't have her new number and I was busy travelling between Britain and the USA. It's so easy to drift apart.

'Then one day I suddenly felt that I'd like to talk to Doris and see how she was. I managed to get her number from *Woman's Own* and I phoned her. We chatted for a while but Doris didn't seem to be all that well. She told me that she'd had a stroke and couldn't manage one of her appearances as a result, and that she'd had cancer before and so on.

'I found myself saying to her over and over again, "Can I help you with anything? If there's anything I can do just let me know," which was crazy because she had everything now. She didn't need any publicity, she didn't need anything from me, but that's all I could think of saying to her.

'Afterwards I thought about what she'd said. She'd insisted that she was going to carry on regardless but underneath that I felt that she was telling me she was going to die.

'Strangely enough, some time before Doris died I was invited to meet another medium. He told me some quite impressive things but towards the end he said something odd.

' "Somebody you know very well is going to die," he said. "She lives in Fulham, or South London or somewhere like that, and she's going to die. But she'll be in touch."

Frank got the strong impression that the medium, who knew nothing about him or his connection with Doris Stokes, was predicting Doris' death. He also felt that when the man mentioned that this woman would be in touch, he meant from the spirit world.

'I'm still waiting,' said Frank. 'I don't know if I like the idea of voices in my ear but perhaps it's not going to be like that. Perhaps being asked to take part in this book is the contact he meant.'

ED DOOLAN
Broadcaster, BBC Radio WM.

It was 6.29 in the evening, and Ed Doolan was busy making the final preparations for his radio show which went out at 6.30, when Doris Stokes walked into the studio.

She sat down opposite him, fixed him with her strikingly-bright blue eyes and proceeded to take his breath away in a couple of short sentences.

' "Don't be uneasy," she told me,' said Ed, "You're not quite happy about this are you?"

' "Well, it is a little strange having someone like you here," I admitted. "After all, if you have the gifts you say you have then it's quite extraordinary."

' "Your father's here, you know," said Doris. "He's got the same name as yours."

'My father had died a few years before in 1970 and he did indeed have the same name.

' "He looks very much like you, you know," Doris went on. "He's laughing and he's very proud of you."

'And at that moment the red light came on and I had to start a phone-in programme.'

Ed struggled to control his conflicting emotions and pilot Doris and the callers smoothly through the show.

'She was brilliant at phone-ins,' said Ed. 'One hundred per cent straight up. I think it was something to do with the fact that it was pure sound and there were no distractions, but throughout all the stuff she was getting for the callers she kept telling me about my father. "He's talking about a birthday," she said. "Why is this birthday important?"

'Well, my father died on my birthday. I was amazed.

'Doris and I got on terribly well. I had her on my programme quite often after that (I was working for Radio BRMB, Birmingham's commercial station, at the time) and we became firm friends. She even stayed at my house a few times.

'I remember one morning after she'd stayed the night she came downstairs and went into the kitchen to have a cup of tea. There she met Liz, the elderly cleaning lady who used to help us out. Liz had quite a few relatives who'd recently died and before she realized what was going on, Doris was getting messages for her from all these recently-departed family members. She was staggered.

'On another occasion, Doris was staying with us the weekend Jocelyn Cadbury, the MP, committed suicide. The police had not yet released the details of how he died but I was interested because I'd met Jocelyn Cadbury. In fact I'd interviewed him only the week before.

'Anyway we were sitting round in the evening chatting, when suddenly Doris said that she'd got Jocelyn Cadbury through. He explained how he'd died. Apparently he'd put a gun in his mouth and pulled the trigger.

'When the details were released to the press we discovered that Doris had been absolutely correct.

'I've seen people make fun of Doris since then but, believe me, when she was good she was quite extraordinary.

'It was always an interesting programme when Doris was on and we got an enormous response, but there was a lot of criticism from religious pressure groups and, unfortunately, commercial stations are much more timid than the BBC. Anyway, on one occasion the BRMB management forbade me to do a phone-in with Doris. They'd caved in to pressure. So instead I invited Doris' fiercest critics on the station, the programme controllers, to sit round the table with me and Doris and do the show that way.

'They agreed. They came in and during the programme Doris potted them off one by one. She went round the table producing all these details about their lives including facts about someone's illegitimate child and someone else's long-lost brother. It was wonderful to sit and watch them squirm.

' "She's very good, isn't she?" they admitted afterwards.'

Above: Doris and John Stokes outside their house –'It was Doris' pride and joy after a lifetime in rented accommodation.'

Below: The Stokes with their great friend, Nancy Sheen, on one of their many journeys round the country.

Derek and Ellen Jameson: close friends and loyal supporters of Doris.

Above: **Doris with her good friend and manager, Laurie O'Leary.** Photograph courtesy of Steve Hickey

Below: **Doris with Tony Ortzen, Editor of *Psychic News* , on stage at Lewisham Theatre.** Copyright Jim Selby

Doris Collins: top medium and colleague of Doris Stokes –'Some time ago, Doris came back to me. . .'

Above: Sally Butten who tragically died in 1984, aged twenty-one.

Below: Doris passed several messages from Sally to her sister, Georgina.

Left: **Comedian Freddie Starr enjoys a joke with Doris on stage at the end of one of her demonstrations.**

Photograph courtesy of Steve Hickey

Above: **Doris with her literary agent, Jenne Casarotto, at the launch party for *Voices of Love* on the Orient Express, November 1986.**

Photograph courtesy of Steve Rapport

Right: Two-year-old Amanda Bringham with her 'Doris dolly'– the doll presented to her by Doris.

Above: Doris and John with Mr and Mrs Bert Weedon. Bert composed some music specially for Doris' record, _Welcome to my World._

Above: Doris was proud to be President of the Cot Death Research Appeal.

Below: Sharing a joke with Jo McDonald, General Secretary of the Appeal.

Not long after this, Ed was invited to join BRMB's rival station in Birmingham, BBC Radio WM. Feeling that the BBC offered him more scope, he accepted and changed situations.

Naturally, Ed wanted to make an impact in his new job and he was soon presented with the perfect opportunity.

'A big row blew up involving Granada Television,' said Ed. 'They had become interested in Doris and had filmed a whole programme featuring Doris working with a live audience. I saw the tape and it was marvellous.

'Doris was pleased with it, too, and she got the impression that the production team was pleased. Then not long afterwards she heard that Granada had decided not to screen the programme.

'The reason they gave was that it showed people crying and was therefore upsetting. Yet anyone could see that the people were crying with happiness and they had given their permission for the material to be used.

'It seemed to me another case of a commercial station bowing to pressure. Fortunately the BBC's not like that. If it's honest and accurate it goes on.

' "OK," I said when I heard what had happened, "We'll have Doris live on the BBC with an audience and it'll go out live over the air. Whatever happens, happens."

'It was arranged very quickly. I announced it at lunchtime one day. We needed 150 people for the studio audience so I asked for people who were interested to apply to the studio by the next morning and the first 150 would be chosen.

'When I arrived the next day there were 700 applications waiting.

'Well, the show was extraordinary. The first ten or fifteen minutes weren't so good but then, suddenly, Doris got hot and she was brilliant. The best I think she's ever done.

'We were both very pleased afterwards. It went so well. But, of course, by then the pressure groups got started and there was hell to pay. It was a great controversy but the BBC management backed me all the way.

'I continued to see a lot of Doris after that. When she was appearing on stage in Birmingham she often asked me to front her shows, which I was glad to do. When I didn't see her I spoke to her frequently on the phone and I visited her in hospital after she'd had a nasty cancer operation.

'We were friends, but friends can sometimes fall out and we even had a row once. I remember I'd invited her to come on the show, as I often did, but on this occasion Doris must have been coming to me from another station where they'd sprung a hostile vicar on her at the last moment.

' "I don't want any vicars on," she said firmly.

'Well, I could understand how she felt but I wasn't having Doris Stokes tell me how to run my programme. As it happened, I hadn't yet decided on the format of the show but that wasn't the point. We did it my way or not at all, and I told her so.

'Doris was a bit miffed and the upshot was that we didn't do the programme. I went on the air and told the listeners what had happened.

'But I knew it wouldn't be a permanent rift. It was one of those things that happen between friends and six months later Doris phoned me as if nothing had happened to see how I was.'

Such a strong bond developed between Ed and Doris that on one occasion when he was taken ill in Birmingham, Doris, miles away in London, knew within minutes.

'It was a bitterly cold night,' said Ed. 'I hadn't long come back from visiting Doris in London. I'd been to the studio and the weather was so bad – there was snow on the ground and the roads were very icy – that I decided to leave the car at the BBC and walk back.

'It was extremely cold and the journey was uphill all the way. By the time I got home I had a terrible pain in my chest. I'd developed angina.

'I went in and lay on the bed feeling desperately ill. I hadn't been there five minutes when the phone rang. It was Doris.

' "Hello, Ed, are you all right, dear?" she asked.

' "No, Doris, I'm not," I told her.

' "No, you're not, are you," she said. "Now, don't panic. Lie quietly and get your breath. You'll be all right."

Ed tried to do as she suggested.

'But, Doris,' he asked weakly, 'why did you phone?'

'Don't be silly, dear,' she said.

Ed did recover on that occasion, just as Doris said he would, but his condition eventually led to a triple bypass operation which has now given him a new lease of life.

'I must have known Doris for near enough ten years and it was well known that we were friends,' said Ed. 'So shortly after the news came out that Doris had died, I got a call from *Central Weekend*, the TV show. They'd decided to talk about whether Doris was straight or not, and knowing that I'd worked with her a great deal they wanted to have me along.

'Now I'd seen this programme before and I thought it was awful. They usually have a couple of experts and lots of people in the audience shouting. They try to do too much and nothing is resolved. I knew the programme wouldn't be good and I heard that they were going to have a clairvoyant on who claimed to be a special friend of Doris' but I happened to know that Doris didn't even respect this particular person.

'I felt I had to go along there and speak up for Doris because they hadn't got anyone else there who knew her well.

'Well, it was as bad as I'd expected. The clairvoyant was in another room. He talked a bit about Doris and then he went off the subject and started to do a bit of mind reading. It was a complete waste of time.

'Eventually they came to me and asked me if I thought she was genuine. At this point I congratulated Central Weekend on winning the Bad Taste Award of the year with double laurels.

' "The woman is still lying in a mortuary in London," I said. "You have a man here she does not even respect. It's appalling bad taste." '

Not surprisingly, the interviewer backed off, but Ed was glad he'd gone along to put his point of view.

These days he still misses those comfortable telephone chats and he still stands up for Doris.

'I thought she was wonderful. When Doris was in the room you felt at one with her. You felt at peace with Doris. I wouldn't say she was always right but, by God, she wasn't often wrong. She was the best of the bunch, no doubt about it.

'I know people have said unpleasant things about her but since my operation I've had a different outlook on life. I know that it doesn't matter what people say. The truth is the truth and people who have been helped by Doris – they know what she did and that's all that matters.

'These days people still ask me if she was genuine.

' "I don't know," I tell them. "To me she was." '

VICKY MAYER
Features Editor, *MS London* Magazine

Vicky Mayer was pretty sceptical the first time she met Doris Stokes. Just twenty-one years old and working for a teenage magazine she was interested enough in psychic phenomena to want to know more, but she was certainly not going to swallow everything she was told.

'I thought I'd go along and see what happened,' said Vicky. 'Doris was absolutely huge then and I read all her books but I didn't really have any preconceived ideas.

'Anyway we started doing the interview and she was answering my questions and giving me some good quotes which was great but I was a bit sceptical about some of the stories she told me about this person and that person.

'Everything was going fine when, halfway through our conversation, she got up and said she was going to the loo. I thought, fine, and sat there and after a moment or two she came back.

' "Does the name Betty mean anything to you?" she asked. "She's about your age."

'And I thought, OK, I see. She's trying to pick some names out of a hat for me. But really. Betty! It's such an old fashioned name to someone of my generation. If she'd said Sharon or something like that, she might have got somewhere. It would have been so much more plausible.

' "No," I said, "I'm afraid it doesn't."

' "Well, I've got a Betty here who's your age. She says she's come as a way of introducing me to you and she wants to talk."

' "I'm sorry," I said, "it doesn't mean a thing. I don't know her."

'Doris just sort-of said, Oh, and left it at that. We went back to the interview.

'I didn't think any more of it. After all, the name Betty didn't mean a single thing to me. I thought Doris was just trying to prove something to me because I was there.

'Anyway a few weeks later my father forced me to go along to this big family gathering. I've got one of those big spread-out families with thousands of great aunts and people like that who I haven't seen since I was a baby. I didn't really want to go but it was a mass visit and my father said you and your sisters have got to come.

'Well, we went off down to Kent where most of the relatives lived and I walked in and one of these great aunts who I'd never met in my life absolutely freaked out when she saw me.

' "It's Betty! It's Betty!" she kept saying, and she was shaking like a leaf.

'I couldn't believe what was going on. "Are you all right?" I asked.

'But she kept staring at me as if I was a ghost and muttering, "Betty!"

'It turned out that her daughter Betty had died twenty years before of a brain haemorrhage when she was twenty-one – the same age as me – and I was the absolute image of her.

'Everyone in the family is very dark except me. I'm blonde and so, apparently, was Betty. It wasn't just the hair colouring though. Apparently we seemed identical in every way. I could have been Betty's twin.

'It was so freaky that it really changed my mind about Doris and set me thinking. I mean, I'd never heard of Betty before.

'Up until then I hadn't really thought about life after death. I'm not a particularly religious person. I don't specially believe in God or Jesus Christ but after meeting Doris I sat down to think about what I actually believe. I realized that it seemed to me that there *is* something after this life. I just feel it in my bones. There is something about and perhaps there are ghosts and spirits. Doris just reinforced my instincts.

'I met her again sometime afterwards at the launch of one of her books. It was pretty crowded but I managed to have a few words with her and I told her about Betty and how I discovered that her message for me had been right all along.

'Doris didn't seem at all surprised. Apparently, this sort of thing happened quite often. She didn't actually say I told you so but she could have done.

'I know there are a lot of people going round saying she was a fake but I had to believe her after that. Mind you, I do think there are a lot of people who want to believe and they are therefore receptive to mediums and they try to fit everything a medium says to their own lives.

'On the other hand there are also people who are very sceptical. They can sometimes be given information that is correct and they say things like, "I don't know how you got that but . . ." and they still won't believe it. You just can't convince them.

'Funnily enough, I expected Doris to come across as far more religious than she did. She didn't seem particularly religious yet she was trying to help people a hell of a lot. She had devoted her life to it and it seemed sad because she was quite ill at the time but she was still trying really hard.

'She showed me the bags of letters she got from various people and that got to me. I wouldn't have liked to be in her position. It must have been like being an agony aunt because she had to take so many people's problems on her shoulders. I don't think I could have coped with that.

'When she was telling me some of the stories, I thought I wouldn't want that for myself. It must have been a difficult life. I'm sorry that I never did get to see her on stage. I always wanted to but somehow I never got round to it.

'I've missed my chance now, which is a shame. I would love to have seen how she coped with those big theatres.'

LINDA BROOKS
Freelance Journalist

It was a party game, nothing more. One night after a jolly dinner, journalist Linda Brooks, her husband, Richard, and two friends, Linda and Martin thought it would be fun to hold a seance.

They arranged a set of alphabet cards in a circle on the table, put an upturned glass in the centre and merrily placed their fingers on the base of the glass.

It was little more than a joke. They weren't expecting anything to happen but as they sat laughing and chatting, the glass began to move under their hands.

'I know it was a silly thing to do,' said Linda. 'Anyway, it was all jokey at first but then something came through very powerfully. We'd ask questions and the glass would answer them. We were all friends and we trusted each other. We knew that none of us was pushing the glass. Something, call it a spirit or what you will, was moving that glass.

'Anyway, after a few questions we asked who we were talking to. The glass moved to the letter L, then A, then R and so on until it had spelled out the word 'Larry'. We were amazed.

'Sometime before that, Richard had lost his best friend. He was a steward on board the plane, Papa India, that crashed in Staines. He was only in his very early twenties when he died and his nickname was Larry. Martin knew him too.

'At first, Richard didn't believe it and kept asking all sorts of difficult questions that only Larry could have answered.

' "What was the name of the butcher's shop we used to work in?"

'Back came the answer. "Viscount."

'Still Richard wasn't satisfied. "What was the name of the nightclub where we worked as waiters?"

'The glass spelled out the name. "The Locarno." This too was correct.

'And so it went on until at last at three in the morning we were too exhausted to go on.

' "Should we see a medium?" Richard asked.

'Back came the answer, "Yes." '

'So sometime after our séance, Richard and Martin went along to the Spiritualist Association and had a sitting with one of the mediums. Unfortunately it didn't go too well and they came away disappointed.'

That would probably have been the end of the idea. But a couple of years later Linda chanced to meet Doris Stokes.

'I was working as a researcher on *Woman's Own* at

the time,' she said, 'and we'd recently run a feature on Doris. Anyway, she came into the office one day with the features editor and we said hello. She seemed very friendly and I'd heard that she was supposed to be very good so I asked if Richard and I could have a sitting with her.'

In those days before she was famous, Doris was busy but not swept off her feet with work, and it wasn't difficult to arrange a mutually-convenient date.

'We went round to her flat in Fulham one evening after work,' said Linda. 'She certainly wasn't rich, and the block where she lived was a bit depressing really. But the flat itself was homely and *Coronation Street* was playing in the background.

'Doris was very chatty, she never changed but she got into it quite quickly. She explained that she didn't switch off the lights or need a darkened room. She just listened to our voices and got on with it.

'She seemed to be focusing on Richard right from the beginning. Right away, she said. "Who's Alice?"

'Well Alice was an aunt of Richard's who'd died.

' "Alice is showing me drawings and things," she said.

'She got that right, too. Richard is an artist. After that she went on a bit about Disney and saying that Aunt Alice thought Richard ought to work in America.

'This was followed by some names we couldn't recognize. It seemed as if the link was getting weak. Then, suddenly, Aunt Alice must have faded out because Doris said, "I've got a young boy here now and he's laughing a lot. He's got a northern accent."

'Now the point about Richard's friend, who *was* from the North, is that he was one of those charismatic people everyone likes. He was so full of life and always laughing. He'd even got into trouble at school because he laughed so much.

' "It was very, very sudden," Doris went on. "He went over like this!" and she clapped her hands loudly together. Which is how it would have been, I suppose.

"He was falling," she said. "He was falling through the sea." Then she stopped. "No, it wasn't the sea," she said, and she sounded puzzled, "He was falling through the sky."

' "Yes, that's right," said Richard. "He was in an air crash."

' "It was all dark and he was very bitter at first, Ricky," she said. " 'I shouldn't have been there,' he's saying, 'That's why I was so bitter. I shouldn't have been there.' "

'And this was true, too. He shouldn't have been on that flight at all but he was on standby and the steward who should have been on duty hadn't turned up.

'We were very sad to think that he'd been unhappy to start with but Doris didn't dwell on it too much. She must have asked him about the things he and Richard used to do together because she went on.

' "He's going over to you, Richard, there's a light over you and he's saying, 'D'you remember the time we went to Blackpool Tower? We had a lot of laughs . . .' "

'This was amazing. When they were students they decided to climb Blackpool Tower from the outside for a Rag Week stunt to raise money. They went along, had a few drinks, and when they reached the foot of the Tower they realized there was no one watching them but for one woman standing in the rain.

' "We're going to climb the Tower from the outside," they told her.

' "Well, mind you don't fall," she said, and went home.

' It seemed rather pointless after that so they gave up the attempt.

' "I can't say that," Doris went on. "He's swearing a bit, you know. Who's Larry?"

'That was marvellous because Larry was his nickname. He was very small at school. They used to call him Larry the Lamb and the nickname stuck.

' "That's him!" we said.

'There was some more reminiscing about the girls they used to know and the good times they had, then Doris said, "He wants you to go and see Sue."

'Sue was the girl he used to live with.

' "Go and see Sue and tell her that you've been here and that you've been in touch," he said, "and don't forget to go and see my mum."

'Then came a bit that knocked us sideways.

' "He's telling me that he's been to see Martin at his house in Philadelphia," said Doris.

'Now this was the same Martin who'd been at the seance that started the whole thing off. Since then, Martin had gone to live in America and he did in fact have a house in Philadelphia.

'We were amazed. This was absolutely incredible and I think that was the point when we were finally convinced.

'We didn't have a very long sitting because Doris was tired, but towards the end she suddenly turned to me and said, "He was with you last night, you know, and he says he was very pleased because you were looking at his photograph. You were wearing blue.'

'Quite right. Knowing that I would be seeing Doris the next day, I got out some of the old photographs of Richard and Larry and I was looking through them before I went to bed. I was wearing my blue dressing-gown. There was one picture in particular that I liked and I put it out on the mantelpiece so that Richard would see it before he left in the morning.

'Doris even referred to this. "He says, will you put that photograph in a frame and put a rose by it," she said.

'I did as she asked and to this day I've got that framed picture in the room where I work.

'Just as we were leaving, Doris turned to me again.

' "Your father is here," she said, although I hadn't told her that I'd lost my father, "but this young man wanted to come through so much that your father stood aside. 'There was a pause then' she added, "Who's Alan?"

' "That's him," we said, 'His real name was Alan. Larry is his nickname."

' "Oh, that explains it," said Doris, "because they were saying, 'Come on, Alan, we've got to go now.' "

'When we left to go home we were quite elated. All the way back on the train we couldn't stop talking about it. Funnily enough we both had peculiar headaches.

' "I've got such a headache," I said to Richard.

' "So have I," he replied and when we described it to each other we realized it was the same: a tight band right round the front of the head. I asked Doris about it afterwards and she said that it was the spirits trying to get through. Because we hadn't got the powers to receive them when they were trying to reach us we ended up with a headache.'

Linda and Richard were quite satisfied with their sitting and had no plans to visit Doris again. Linda couldn't imagine that she'd ever need to consult a medium.

But things seldom turn out as we plan. Several years later, Linda's much-loved mother died and suddenly Linda needed the sort of comfort that Doris was able to give the bereaved.

This time, though, it wasn't so easy to get a sitting.

'By this time Doris was a world-famous medium and she was very, very busy,' said Linda. 'I couldn't get a sitting just because I wanted one. Fortunately I was working for *19 Magazine* at the time. It was a young woman's magazine and I was able to suggest a feature about the impact Doris had on young people.

'This appealed to Doris because she was interested in reaching the young, so she agreed to see me and I mentioned that I was hoping for a sitting at the end of our interview.

'I didn't tell her why, or who I was hoping to contact, and I don't suppose she remembered me from all those years ago.

'This time I saw Doris at her new house. She was still as warm and nice and friendly as ever but I noticed that she was very sensitive to all the criticism she'd been getting. She kept showing me news-cuttings and things, and she kept talking about the cases of people she'd helped. She'd had a hard time of it and it all seemed unfair because she was genuinely trying to help people.

'Anyway we got on with the interview and she was quite amazed at the number of young people who went to her shows and sent her flowers and so on. She seemed to be a granny figure to them. I got some nice quotes. She told me bits of her life-story too and we talked for a long time.

'Then suddenly she half turned to me and said, "Who's this woman who keeps saying, 'Can I come through now, Doris? Can I come through? I've been waiting a long time?'"

' "I think it must be my mum," I said. I didn't intend to give anything away but I decided to tell her that.

' "She hasn't been over very long," said Doris, "because it's a very little light."

118

'This was true. My mother had only died a few months before.

' "Oh dear, she did suffer," said Doris, "but she's all right now, she's saying."

'Mum was in hospital for three months before she died.

'And it's not an old voice. I'd say she was in her sixties. About sixty-eight perhaps." said Doris.

'In fact, Mum was seventy-six but she was very young for her age and very active. She would have sounded younger than she was.

' "She's going over to you and saying, 'That's my baby,' " said Doris, "so I know you were the youngest."

' "That's right."

'There were a few names after that I couldn't recognize, then she said, "Who's Anne living?"

' "Anne is one of my mum's sisters," I said.

' "She's sending her love to Anne. 'Tell her I'm all right, dear.' "

'Doris seemed to be listening to a conversation I couldn't hear for a few moments, then she said, "Your mum has someone called John with her. She's helping him because he only recently passed."

'I couldn't think of anyone called John but Doris kept on about him.

' "He's talking about someone with a B sound . . . Brenda . . . no, it's not Brenda, it's Brian. He's sending love to Brian."

'That was when I twigged. Brian is my husband's brother-in-law. His father had died just a few days before. His name was John.

' "Now I'm getting a B sound again," said Doris.

' "Is it Brian again?" I asked.

' "No," said Doris, "It's your mum talking and it's Beryl."

'Beryl was Brian's wife.

' "She's saying to tell Beryl not to worry."

'I wasn't sure what this meant. All I could think was that while Mum was in hospital her mind was half-here and half-not-here. She'd had a stroke and she was thinking about Beryl quite a lot because Beryl was in the house when it happened and it upset her to see my mum like that. Perhaps she meant that Beryl shouldn't dwell on that any more and she should remember Mum how she used to be.

'Anyway, all this time she hadn't mentioned my father at all and although I didn't want to give any information away I couldn't help asking about this.

' "Is my mum with my dad?" I asked.

' "Does she mean Ted?" said Doris, though it was obviously Mum speaking to her.

'My dad's name was Ted. I nodded.

' "Of course I'm with Ted. Who d'you think I'm with? He came to meet me. There's nothing to it. I saw him before I came over in my room and I knew that everything was all right."

'Doris was obviously getting something very strong and I was pleased to think that Mum and Dad were together.

'There were a few more names that I couldn't recognize, then Doris started talking about a letter M. A very strong M.

' "That's my little boy, Michael," I said. I gave her that, of course, but I felt she was so close to it I'm sure that's what she was trying to say.

'She started chatting away again to this unseen presence, then she looked puzzled.

' "Did you have a miscarriage?" she asked me.

' No," I said.

' "Well, she's talking about a miscarriage," Doris insisted.

' "Yes, my mum had one."

' "I see," said Doris, still talking to my mum. "And do you mean you called him David, or have you got a David?" she turned back to me.

' "David's my other son," I said.

' "Ah, that's what she means. Don't forget David, she's saying."

'Then she mentioned Ben and two birthdays in April. Both my brother and I have birthdays in April and his name is Len, which is close enough to Ben for me to be able to accept that from Doris.

' "Fondest love to Len," said Doris. "He's very good at figures you know."

'He is. Extremely.

'Then someone else seemed to move in.

' "Your dad's here and he's been over a long time."

' "That's right," I said, "He's been dead for over twenty years."

' "Now that's my Princess, he's saying. 'I'd do anything for my Princess.' "

'That was exactly what he used to call me. His princess. Doris went on about what he'd been doing. He'd been to Australia and so on. Well, he did love travelling so he might have done, I suppose. Some things were absolutely right and others I wasn't sure about. It was as if Doris was picking up the threads of all sorts of bits and pieces and then something would come through and it was clear as anything. After a vague bit my mum seemed to come back.

' "This sounds a bit peculiar," said Doris," but she's talking about someone with a name like Bunny."

' "I don't know who that could be," I said and then suddenly I remembered a man called Bunge whom Mum had known when she was in hospital.

' "Could it be Bunge?"

' "Yes, that's it," said Doris. "He's here with your mum."

'As it happened this Bunge had died just a few days before my meeting with Doris. When Mum was alive he'd tried to help her to get a place in a home for when she came out of hospital.

'She had suffered such a severe stroke that she would have needed total care.

' "Your mum wouldn't have wanted to be in a home," said Doris.

' "Doris, I would have hated it . . . Can you imagine me, listen dear Newton . . ."

' "Newman," I corrected. It was so close.

' "Can you imagine me, Mrs Newman, sitting in a chair with a lot of old dears being taken to the toilet? . . . No, I'm better off with your father. You thought I didn't know but I did. I was bodily ill but not senile."

'It was quite true: Mum would have hated it. She'd been so active.

'There were a few more little details but those were the main things. It was quite a long sitting really and once again, when it was over, I had that strange headache.

'When I left I felt much better. I think Doris was a wonderful person. She helped so many people and I don't think she was trying to delude anyone for a minute. She really believed in what she was doing and, as for me, it definitely helped and comforted me.

'I know so many people, my friends and relatives, who would have given anything to have seen her. I've had to tell my story so many times. They're fascinated.

122

Yet funnily enough, my mum would never have gone to see a medium after my father died. She was distraught but she wouldn't have gone to a medium.

'It worried me a bit. I mean, I wondered whether I ought to be going to see Doris if my mum was against it. But I wanted to go and in the end I decided to follow my own instincts.

'I'm glad I did. It was a great comfort, particularly the thought that my mum and dad are together somewhere.

'I doubt if I'd go to anyone else now. I've seen Doris and I think she was the best. She helped me and I think that, without doubt, she had a special gift.'

BARRY GOMER
Photographer, *Daily Express*

The last thing Barry Gomer expected when he set off for work in May 1985 was that he was about to receive a message from his dead father.

Photographers on the *Daily Express* rarely know what their next assignment is going to be. Stories are usually handed out on the day of the interview so it wasn't until later that morning that Barry learned he would be accompanying the columnist Jean Rook on an interview with Doris Stokes that day.

It was just another job as far as Barry was concerned. It made no difference to him whether he was photographing a medium or a meat-packer. It was the quality of the picture that counted.

What happened is only a tiny incident yet it is typical of the way Doris worked. Most people who came into contact with her, for whatever reason, came away with some tiny snippet that was quite uncanny.

'I'd never been convinced about mediums,' said Barry, 'so I didn't think Doris was going to be anything special. I was going to photograph her and that was it.

'The most unusual thing about the job as far as I was concerned was that it was taking place in Guy's Hospital. Doris had been taken in for tests – I'm not sure what for but she didn't look well. It was unusual to do an interview in hospital but Doris was very busy around that time and it was difficult to fit in another date. While she was at Guy's there was a lot of hanging about waiting for tests so she probably felt it would take her mind off things to talk to Jean in between them.

'Doris was sitting there chatting quite naturally. I liked her. She seemed quite mumsy. Not at all intimidating.

'Jean was talking to her, doing the interview, and after a while Doris said something like, "Someone's trying to get through now." As she was talking to Jean, Doris naturally thought the message was for Jean. "Do you know anyone called Eileen?" she asked.

'Jean said she didn't. The name meant nothing to her. Doris seemed quite sure about it but as Jean couldn't claim it they were about to go on when I couldn't help interrupting.

' "Eileen's my mother," I said.

' "Oh, we've found Eileen," said Doris, very pleased. "Well, I think I've got your father here and he wants you to pass on a message to Eileen."

'I was amazed. My father had died only a year before.

' "Tell her your father's OK and that everything will be all right. She mustn't worry."

'I was staggered. Out of all the thousands of names she could have picked on, to choose Eileen, which was correct, was beyond a fluke. What's more, there's no way she could have known my father had died – in fact

124

there's no way she could have known anything about me.

'Jean seemed quite impressed and I was amazed. It certainly made me think. I told my mother about it afterwards and she found it very comforting. I don't think she'd been worrying about anything specific as far as I know but obviously when you're adjusting to living alone you have more responsibility and more worries.

'That was all Doris got for me, but then she was in the middle of an interview.

'I know she kept mentioning Diana Dors. Apparently Diana Dors, who'd recently died, had been an old friend of hers and Jean knew her too. Doris told Jean she'd spoken to Diana quite a lot since she'd come into hospital. In fact she wasn't worried about the results of her X-rays.

' "I took Diana down to X-ray with me and she said, 'Don't worry. You're clear,' " she told us.

'It turned out she was right.

'I don't think I'd ever seen a medium before I met Doris and I've never seen one since. I don't suppose I would seek one out but I must say, Doris was an extraordinary lady.'

BEL AUSTIN
Senior Reporter, Kent Messenger Group

When reporter Bel Austin was invited to the launch of Doris Stokes' latest book, *Voices of Love*, which took place aboard the Orient Express, she accepted of course – who wouldn't? But she also took her camera along to record the event. After all, who knew when she might get another chance to ride the legendary train.

And as the Express roared through the dreary November afternoon, Bel roamed the rosewood carriages with their marquetry panels, art-deco lights and small tables gleaming with white linen, lead crystal and heavy silver, snapping pictures as she went.

The afternoon was exciting and glamorous. Nothing spooky about it. Yet when Bel had her photographs developed she noticed something strange.

'I took about fifteen snaps of various celebrities, including two of Doris. Doris was moving about chatting to people yet when the pictures came out you could see a light shining quite clearly over Doris' head in both shots. It couldn't have been simply a reflection in the wood veneer because Doris wasn't in the same place for both pictures and the light didn't appear over anyone else. I've got pictures of Derek Jameson and John Inman standing beside the panelling but there is no light above them.

'I showed the pictures to a lot of people and they agree that it's most odd.'

Bel first met Doris when she went to interview her. She heard that Doris had bought a holiday home on the Isle of Sheppey which was within the area she covered for her paper and she asked if she could write a story about it. Doris agreed, but since she wasn't actually staying on Sheppey at the time, Bel set off for the medium's home in South London where Doris said they could talk in peace.

'Doris lived in a very pretty house which the experts from *Woman's Own* had helped her to design and decorate internally,' said Bel. 'When I arrived the doctor had just left and Doris was sitting on a rubber ring which had been placed over the top of the cushion on her armchair. Apparently she was suffering from an arthritic condition and the ring helped take the pressure off her spine.

'She was a large lady, even sitting down – a much bigger person than I'd expected, with very penetrating blue eyes. Yet there was nothing frightening about her. She was like someone's favourite auntie.

'She'd obviously suffered a lot of ill-health and wasn't very well but she was quite cheerful about it. She joked that she'd lost so many bits and pieces through operations that when it was her time to go over she'd collect them all up in a carrier bag at the door!

'She'd just rescued a little dog called Boots, who was jumping about, and this turned out to be significant. I'd had to take my dog with me that day and although Doris liked dogs it wasn't possible to take him into the house because of Boots. This was perfectly all right, I thought. My dog would be fine in the car. But the interview went on much longer than I expected and after a while Doris started asking me who Tom was. She kept on and on about this Thomas or Tom. At first I couldn't think who she meant; I was thinking of a person. Then I remembered my dog Tom sitting outside in the car. She went on about Tom so much I went out to see if he was all right and I found him absolutely gasping.

'It was a warm day and the car had got very hot. Apparently he could have died in seven minutes of extreme heat and I dread to think what would have happened if Doris hadn't given me that warning.'

Bel had gone to see Doris in order to interview her, not to press for a sitting, but as often happened, Doris began to hear voices during the conversation.

'She mentioned the names Lilian and Tony,' said Bel, 'both of them known to me. Then she went on to describe my daughter correctly, right down to her colouring, my own domestic situation and also my mother's illness.

'This was quite extraordinary because I hadn't given her a single clue about myself or my family.

'I wasn't a believer when I went but I came away thinking that something strange had just happened.

'There was no way she could have known anything about me and I certainly didn't give anything away during the interview. We were talking about Doris, not me.'

Bel went back to her office and wrote a long feature about the encounter, which so pleased Doris that she invited Bel to the Orient Express celebrations.

'It was a wonderful experience,' said Bel.

These days Doris remains as popular as ever on the Isle of Sheppey.

'You can never pick up any of her books in the library,' said Bel. 'There's always a waiting list. Some people are sceptical of course, but for every sceptic there are a thousand fans.'

GARTH PEARCE
Show Business Editor, *Daily Express*

It was a story in the *Los Angeles Times* that caught Garth Pearce's eye. Garth, an ambitious young journalist covering show business for the *Daily Express* visited Los Angeles three or four times a year to look round Hollywood and interview the stars.

But the story that interested him didn't concern any star. It was about an obscure British housewife who had somehow managed to impress the hard-bitten cynics of LA with some psychic information about a boy who had died.

128

'According to the paper this lady came from Fulham,' said Garth, 'and her name was Doris Stokes. This was 1979 and I'd never heard of Doris Stokes but I wanted to know more. From a show-business point of view an ordinary British woman going into the heart of LA – a town that's seen it all before, full of people who're not easy to impress – and managing to make an impact, is pretty amazing.

'I was cynical about mediums but this woman had succeeded where thousands of would-be starlets had failed and I wanted to meet her and find out how she'd done it. When I got home I phoned her and arranged an interview.

'Doris seemed to be a warm friendly woman. We started talking about her life and the first thing that happened was that the tape-recorder wouldn't work. I discovered afterwards that she often had this effect on tape-recorders.

'Anyway we carried on and then suddenly, in the middle of answering questions about herself, Doris asked: "Who's Edith?"

'This was my grandmother's name. She died ten years before.

' "Edith's telling me about your house," said Doris. "She's showing me the dining-room. There are french windows overlooking the terrace and she's pointing to a photograph on the wall to one side of the french windows."

'This was an accurate description of my dining-room apart from the photograph.

' "No, there's no photograph on the wall in the dining-room," I said.

'Then I remembered that in fact we had a print of Lichfield in that position and Lichfield was my grandmother's home town.

' "Who's Denis?" Doris went on.

'Denis is my father's name. She then gave me the names Betty, Nell and Chrissie all in a row. These are my father's sisters.

' "She's telling me that your parents are having an extension built on their kitchen," said Doris.

'This was absolutely correct.

'Doris mentioned my daughter, Gemma, and also the name Min. Now Min is an unusual name but earlier that day I had been talking to a publicist whose assistant was called Min.

There were other pieces of jumbled information which meant nothing to me but I relayed them to my mother afterwards and they turned out to be quite accurate.

'I was very impressed. I had arrived in a cynical frame of mind and I said very little. I certainly didn't give Doris any information about myself. Yet there was no way she could possibly have done any research on me and come up with the things she did.

'She also turned round to the photographer who was with me and told him something private about someone very close to him who had died. I think he found it extremely comforting when he got over his surprise.

'I was amazed. I wrote a feature for the *Express* and the response was enormous. We had a tremendous number of letters pouring in. So many people wanted comfort and Doris comforted thousands.

'People who criticized her without knowing her didn't know what they were saying. They forgot about the good she did.

'I don't think she was ever malicious or vindictive. If she made a mistake it was in putting herself in a situation where she had to perform. Yet I don't think she was really bothered about money. When I met her she was charging £8 a sitting (she was the breadwinner of the family), yet she had played the Sydney Opera House and she could have charged what she liked after that. She was naive about money and not trying to make a profit out of what she did.

'I met Doris again some time later and I felt that if she'd had a wider education she would have been able to interpret far more exactly and intelligently. I think she often picked things up that she couldn't put into perspective.

'Since then I've interviewed most of the major names in show business, Redford, Newman, Selleck, and now I realize just what a remarkable person Doris was. She had an extra something that even those big stars didn't have. A natural magnetism that could fill the Sydney Opera House yet was just as effective on a one-to-one basis.

'Doris proved to me that there is an extra dimension. I don't know what it is – but it's there.'

Working With Doris

LAURIE O'LEARY

On Laurie O'Leary's desk in his East-End office there stands a very special photograph. It is a picture of his late mother. Nothing particularly unusual about that, you might think, but to Laurie – Doris Stokes' former manager – it has a unique significance.

For twenty years he was unable even to glance at his mother's face, let alone display her photograph. Yet now, thanks to Doris, he has been able to visit her grave for the first time in two decades and he is happy to have her picture close at hand as a constant reminder.

'I'd known and worked with Doris for some time when it happened,' said Laurie. 'She'd told me a few extraordinary things over the months but I'd never had a sitting. I could have done, of course, but there were so many desperate people I didn't think it would be right. They were more in need than I was. If I'd taken advantage of my position with Doris it would have been out of curiosity, and that would have been unforgivable when I was having to turn away desperate people because Doris just couldn't physically see them all.

'Anyway, one day I was at her home and we were talking, probably about a forthcoming tour or demonstration or something. After a while we strayed off the subject and something was said about families.

' "My mother was quite a nice-looking lady, you know, Doris," I said.

'And instead of answering she looked at me with a look that seemed to stare straight through me.

' "She'll box your ears, son," she said at last.

' "What d'you mean?" I asked.

'Doris didn't answer directly at first.

' "She *is* a nice-looking lady. You're right," she said.

' ."Yes, all right, Doris. She's a nice-looking lady. But what d'you mean?"

' "She's standing by your shoulder, smiling away."

'Doris often said that, in later life, she only saw spirit children, but in fact she did sometimes see adults too and this seemed to be one of those occasions.

' "Yes, she's not a bit like you, you know. She's a slim lady. Very nice-looking, I'd say, with jet-black, shiny hair and a gypsy face."

'This was my mother to a tee and there was no way Doris could have known that I took after my father and had no resemblance to my mother at all. But why should my mother want to box my ears?

' "She says she's pleased you're working with me," Doris went on, "but one thing angers her. You keep getting that photograph out of the third drawer down and putting it back again. 'Don't be ashamed of me, love,' she says. 'Get out some photographs and put flowers by them.' "

'Well, I went absolutely cold. I couldn't believe it. I'd had a photo of my mum since she had gone over twenty years before and I couldn't bear to look at it. I kept it in the third drawer down of the dressing-table – face-down at the bottom so that I was never in danger of forgetting it was there and seeing my mum's face by accident when I went to get something out.

'Every now and then when I was clearing the drawer out and looking at old things, I'd think what's that? And I'd turn it over without thinking and come face-to-face with my mum. It gave me the shivers. I'd accepted my mother's death and I knew she'd gone, but I still got the shivers when I saw that photo. I'd put it back quickly and I wouldn't see it again for years until the next time I had a turn-out.

'But after Doris gave me that message I was able to get that picture out and put it on my desk. I often say, "Hello, Mum," now and sometimes if I've got a problem I'll say, "What shall I do, Rose? D'you really think I'm doing the right thing?" – because I feel she's not far away.

'I was also able to visit her grave. I'd been worried because I'd never been able to face going. I hadn't been since the funeral. This seemed to be the right time to mention it to Doris.

' "You know, Doris, I don't even go to see my mother's grave," I said, "I just couldn't. I've never been there since the day she was buried."

'And Doris said something that was very important to me.

' "But it doesn't matter, Laurie. You don't have to go to the grave if you don't want to. If it gives you comfort fine, I don't tell people not to go, but it's not important. I mean after all, when we went to Grantham I didn't go to see my John Michael's grave (John Michael was Doris' baby son who died at five months old) or my parent's grave."

.And I thought about it and realized that this was true. When we'd visited Grantham while we were in the area for a theatre demonstration, Doris hadn't even mentioned these graves.

' "No, Doris, you didn't," I admitted.

' "That's because my parents and John Michael aren't there, love," she said. "We only buried their old over-coats. I didn't need to go to the church to be with my son. He's with me every day."

134

'I was taken aback yet totally captivated at the same time. I found it very comforting. I went home and got out that photo and not long afterwards I was able to visit my mother's grave.'

These days Laurie O'Leary is one of Doris Stokes' staunchest supporters. Well over a year since her death, he still regards himself as working for her memory and he continues to answer the letters from Stokes fans which even now find their way to his office.

Yet the first time he saw Doris he was a sceptic, convinced that she must be a fraud, and he set out to expose her.

'A friend of ours called Maureen had a couple of tickets for a Doris Stokes demonstration at Walthamstow and she invited my wife along,' said Laurie. 'Iris thought Doris was a fortune-teller and so she agreed to go, but as the date drew nearer she realized she'd been wrong. I could see she was worried.

' "Well, someone told me she talks to the dead," she admitted, "and I don't want to talk to the dead. The trouble is I've said I'll go. Would you go instead of me?"

'She really didn't want to go so I said I'd go in her place. I'd never heard of Doris Stokes and I had no reason to contact the dead. I had no interest in psychic things at all. I'd been in the music business. I'd been a promoter and I worked with a lot of famous pop stars, real household names. But Doris Stokes meant nothing to me.

When I arrived at Walthamstow I saw lots of people queuing outside. There were so many in fact that I thought I must have come to the wrong place. When I checked though, I found it was the right place and I was impressed. As I was going in I even saw a girl I knew whose husband had recently died.

' "What are you doing here?" she asked.

135

' "Probably the same as you're doing," I said. I didn't twig that perhaps she was hoping to get a message from her husband. I thought she'd come out of curiosity like me.

'Anyway, Maureen finally arrived and we went into the hall. The stage was very stark and bare. There was a table rather like a kitchen table with two chairs on either side of it and a little posy on the top, and I thought, "Oh God, are we going to sing hymns?" It was a bit like the local Methodist Church. I didn't feel right at all. I was sure I was wasting my time.

' "What are we doing here, Maureen?" I asked her. "Why did you want to come?"

'Maureen told me she'd read one of Doris' books and was intrigued. She'd had a tough time recently. She'd had a major operation and it started her thinking about things she'd previously been too busy to consider. Anyway, she wanted to see the lady who'd written all these things.

'Just then, Nancy Sheen (a friend of Doris') came on. At least *she* seemed like a normal person. She announced Doris Stokes, and Doris walked on in her long dress. She wasn't at all what I expected.

' "Hello, loves," she said in a warm friendly way which relaxed me. She seemed normal, too.

'She told a few jokes and then she got started with these messages. Well, I was sure the whole thing was a set-up. The people must be plants. There was one woman who got several things. She kept bleating, "Yeees, Doris," and I thought, "Oh God, not her again. She must know everybody in this so-called spirit world." Yet despite that, Doris had such a presence on stage that she held my attention the whole evening.

'Afterwards, in the car going home, I asked Maureen what she thought.

136

' "What did *you* think, Laurie?" she asked.

' "Well, they're planted, those people," I said. "It's obvious. They've got to be plants. I mean, if what she's doing is true, it's absolutely marvellous and she's a marvellous lady, but if not, then she's a very wicked woman and I'd like to expose her."

' "Supposing she's genuine?" asked Maureen.

' "If she's honest – well, if she's honest I'd like to manage her."

' "You don't even know her," said Maureen, as much as to say that's a bit over the top, but I was serious.

'Afterwards, I went back to the pub I run and, of course, they all took the mickey out of me. "Let's have some spirits! Buy us a round!" and all that. But Maureen gave me a copy of one of Doris' books and I read it. I was intrigued and impressed. I thought, "She can't write a book like this if it's all lies."

'By coincidence Ronnie Kray's mum had died. I'd known the Krays for years. We grew up together in the East End and though I wasn't interested in leading the type of life they led, I'd kept in touch. Anyway, knowing how fond of his mum Ronnie had been, I sent him a copy of Doris' book in prison. I thought it might comfort him. Not long afterwards he wrote back saying he'd like to meet this Doris Stokes.'

Now Laurie O'Leary had an excuse to get in touch with Doris. He contacted the tour promoters who agreed to ask Doris if she would talk to him. Doris said she would.

'I explained that I'd been to the show and read her books and I would very much like to meet her,' said Laurie. 'Also I said, "If it's interesting to you, I've given your book to Ronnie Kray, one of the infamous Kray brothers, and he would like to see you."

' "Would he, love," said Doris. "What on earth for?"

137

' "Well, I knew him as a kid, Doris," I explained. "Of course, I'm not a villain but I'm an East-Ender and we grew up together. Now, Ronnie's a villain but he loved his mother and she passed recently. He was so impressed with your book he wanted to see you and hear more." '

Doris didn't care what people had done in the past, it was what they made of their lives now that counted and the fact that a hard man such as Ronnie Kray was interested in spiritualist philosophy seemed a hopeful sign. She agreed to visit him in prison.

'She described the visit and her sitting with Ronnie in one of her books, 'said Laurie. 'I went with her and of course it gave me a chance to meet her properly. I was even more intrigued. I thought, she couldn't be lying, could she? I wanted to know and I wanted to test her. I had some spare time just then so I asked if I could travel with her at my own expense. If she was dishonest, I wanted to find out and I would expose her.

' "All right," said Doris, who always enjoyed having people round her. "You can travel with me if you want to."

'The first thing we did was visit a spiritualist church at Stevenage. It was a 600-seater and it was full. We got a warm welcome. Doris appeared on stage and she was convincing. I kept looking to see if she had things up her cuff or sleeve and I looked around for any signs of a set-up. I thought I was being discreet. It wasn't until three theatres later I realized she'd seen through me.

' "You're checking on me, aren't you, Laurie," said Doris one night.

' "Not checking, Doris," I said. "Well, checking for myself, I suppose."

' "D'you want to follow me to the loo?"

' "No!" I thought she was joking but she wasn't.'

' "That's what a reporter did," she said. "He'd been commissioned to write a story. He'd been with me the whole time before a demonstration and he wanted to see if I destroyed anything in the loo before I went on stage. So he came with me, and I don't want to be rude, but he sort of looked throughout!"

By this time I was with Doris backstage, either driving her or being driven with her to theatres. I was observing very closely what she was doing and I was listening to the comments of the people as they came out of the theatre. I could see that she was obviously very good for the people and I wasn't as sceptical as I had been. I realised that she couldn't possibly have memorized all the things that were happening and I began looking at her in a different light.

' "Doris, I realize you don't have a manager," I said to her one day, "And you need one."

' "Why?" asked Doris.

' "Because you can't possibly cope with all this," I said. "Look what's happening to you. I could manage you and it wouldn't cost you anything."

' "How can you work without being paid?" Doris asked.

' "Well, I'll promote you," I said. "I've been a promoter for many years. My promotions will give me sufficient funds to live on and I won't charge you for management."

' "Isn't it too grand for me to have a manager?" asked Doris.

' "No, it isn't," I said, "but you can say I'm your promoter, if you'd rather."

'Doris agreed because she did need the help, and I said, "Right. No more are you going to have to travel by train, unless you want to. You'll be picked up by car and you'll be driven wherever you need to go. I'll look after your welfare as if you were a star because in my opinion you are a star."

"That was in 1984 and we worked together until she passed.

'We used to talk a lot, Doris and I, and she answered all my questions.

'One day, I said, "What about this talking to the dead? Do you think it's right?"

' "Of course, love," she replied. "I don't talk to them unless they want to talk to me."

'I believe in God, but Doris didn't destroy my image of God or Jesus.

' "Yes, there is a spirit world which will be your heaven," she said. "There's no hellfire as such. You don't go stoking the fires if you've been bad, but you do go to a different, bleaker place."

'She was very well-read on the Bible and I was impressed by her answers to religious critics.

' "If they're that good, why aren't they preaching their own religion instead of trying to stop me preach mine?" she said. "They quote the Bible and quote the Bible. I believe in the Bible but I also know it has been rewritten so many times, who knows how much is right? I think you should believe what seems right to you and come to God in your own way."

'It all seemed logical to me and I was no longer sceptical. I thought what she was doing was marvellous. She was helping people who were in total despair.

'All the time I was discovering just how good she was. On one occasion, some people I knew were in the theatre. The woman had lost her husband in very violent, tragic circumstances and she was desperate to get a message from him. Unknown to me, they'd twice been to see Doris without getting a message and a couple of times I got them tickets because I felt sorry for them.

'I said nothing to Doris about it. I didn't want to take advantage by pushing them in front of other people just because I knew them. So I got them tickets and left things at that. It was in the lap of the gods as far as I was concerned.

'Well, on their last visit, the fourth demonstration they'd been to, it was getting near the end of the evening and nothing had happened. Doris was tired and she was finishing off the Question Time when a girl stood up and said: "Doris, this lady here is in absolute despair and grief. Can't you help her?"

' "Yes, I know, love," said Doris, and gave her a complete sitting there and then. She got the circumstances absolutely right.

' "I'm getting a bang and . . . pain . . . Is it a stabbing? No, I've been shot!" she said. "Oh, God . . ."

'And she went on to describe the incident: How it happened beside a car in a pub carpark. Everything was absolutely accurate.

'I was amazed and very impressed. I knew that Doris knew nothing about it at all. She didn't know these people, yet she was right in everything.

'That's why I get so incensed when people say Doris was a fraud. I defy anyone to go on stage for two hours and keep people occupied by lying and cheating. Not just once, but over and over again.

'If she was a fraud, then I had to be a fraud because Doris couldn't have done it alone. They say we planted people which is totally untrue. Sometimes I sit back thinking, is it worth it? But then I have to challenge people who say Doris was a fraud because I know she wasn't.

'Since she passed, several people have approached me. I've been offered a sizeable fee to expose Doris Stokes. But I couldn't do it even if I wanted to. There's nothing to expose.

'The last time I saw Doris was on the morning of her operation. She phoned and asked me to go to the hospital. When I arrived she sort-of looked at me.

' "All right Doris?" I asked.

'She said no.

' "You're not all right?"

' "No, I'm bitter."

' "All the years I've been with you, you've convinced me there's a spirit world," I said, "and you're afraid of dying, Doris Stokes?"

' "Afraid of dying? Don't be so silly," she said, 'You know I'm not afraid of dying. No, what I'm afraid of is what if it goes wrong? It's a very delicate operation. If it goes wrong what good would I be to anybody? I wouldn't be able to work and that's all I do, isn't it? If I can't do that, Laurie, what good would I be?"

' "Doris Stokes, you've done too much good for the spirit world for them to do that to you," I said. "And on the other hand, if you do leave us and go into the spirit world, please don't put voices in my ear. I don't want them! I can manage you as a medium but *I* don't want to be a medium!"

'Well, she burst out laughing and I laughed with her. Just then they came to get her ready for the operation. I had to go, of course, and so that's the last memory I have of her. She was laughing.

'Since then I've done everything I can to keep the Doris Stokes name going. She was a very special person. Still is, you see. When I talk to people they think I'm crazy talking about Doris as if she was still here. They don't understand that she hasn't really left. I still

142

feel her around. As far as I'm concerned, Doris Stokes is still my friend.'

TONY ORTZEN

These days Tony Ortzen, Editor of the *Psychic News*, can truthfully boast that he has appeared on stage at the London Palladium. He's appeared at a number of other famous theatres too.

It's not that Tony discovered any previously unsuspected talents – it was simply the unexpected result of a long association with Doris Stokes.

Back in the seventies when Tony was still a reporter he became one of the first members of the press to interview Doris in the days before she was a household name. They became friends and later, when Doris needed someone to introduce her on stage to her audience, she thought of Tony.

Tony wasn't always available, of course, but when he could spare the time he was glad to help.

'I started out at *Psychic News* sixteen years ago as a reporter,' he said. 'In those days, although Doris was known in spiritualist circles, she hadn't made any impact on the public. With the greatest respect she was an ordinary medium going out to the churches just like a lot of other mediums.

'But she loved being on the telephone even then and she phoned the office regularly from her home in Lancaster to talk and talk. She loved a chat. I remember being amazed when she had her breast operation. She phoned just a few days later and she was fighting fit. I've never forgotten that. She spoke to me and my colleague.

'She was very excited because she planned to come to London to work at the SAGB and once she arrived I had to go and interview her. Although we'd spoken on the phone so often, we'd never met and I was a bit nervous.

'Doris and John were living in a flat for disabled ex-servicemen. I remember Doris describing it jokingly as being like Sing Sing. With the greatest respect to the residents currently living there, it wasn't the nicest of places in those days. There were lots of concrete stair-ways and iron balconies, and I'm sure at that stage they didn't even have a bathroom.

'I suppose the point I'm trying to make is that for many years Doris had struggled away with her clairvoy-ance for peanuts. She earned virtually nothing. Any-way, I interviewed her and she gave me a sitting. Frankly, it wasn't remarkable. I was very young and there were odds and ends that were quite right but it wasn't dramatic. Nevertheless she certainly struck me as very homely, warm and honest.

'Some time after that an Australian TV producer came to this country and asked if I could recommend a good medium to appear on a programme he was making.

' "Well," I said, "there's a very good medium called Doris Stokes who recently moved to London from the North of England."

'I thought of Doris because she was very chatty, very warm and I thought she'd be good on television. Some mediums are good in churches but they dry up in front of a camera. Doris, I felt, would cope with a camera as well as she could cope with an audience. She might be trembling away inside, and later on she might be trembling physically because of ill-health, but she would come across as very confident, very calm, very collected. Totally in control of the situation.

'Well, Doris did that TV interview and as a result of it she was invited to Australia where she was a great success and ended up touring the country and appearing at the Sydney Opera House.

'While she was there she phoned me several times to tell me how things were going and she sent Australian press cuttings to the office. They were very good. She was certainly attracting a lot of attention there and I believe *Psychic News* became the first British paper to report on her Australian tour.

'Before she'd left Britain she was writing her first book and I remember that when we were talking on the phone one day she asked me what I thought she should call it.

' "I'll have a think about it," I promised. "I can't come up with a title off the top of my head."

'A little while later I was lying in the bath, or washing up or doing something mundane, when the idea suddenly came into my head: "Voices in My Ear" – because Doris was a clairaudient, she heard voices. I phoned Doris to tell her and that was the title that was eventually chosen.

'When the book came out, Doris gave me a gold identity bracelet as a thankyou gift.

'A couple of years later when another of her books was being launched, she phoned me out of the blue to ask if I could help again.

'We're having a river-trip down to Greenwich," said Doris, "and afterwards there's going to be a demonstration at the local theatre. Would you chair it for me?"

'Now I'd never chaired a meeting before and I was really quite apprehensive about it. Some of Fleet Street's top journalists were going to be there. But I agreed and we got a coach down from Greenwich to the theatre and, whilst my legs weren't shaking before I went on, I certainly felt a bit trembly and I could detect a vague tremor in my hand.

'Doris seemed quite happy about it though and she asked me to help out again and again. In fact, I've lost count of the number of times I've chaired her meetings. I did the Palladium, the Dominion – a great many famous theatres. It's funny, we went to the Palladium a number of times and I thought to myself, I never dreamed I'd be sitting on stage at the London Palladium one day.

'Quite frankly though, the Palladium is a beautiful theatre but from the stage it's quite claustrophobic. It's rather high and the circle and the gods seem to loom over you.

'It's quite exciting sitting on stage but I remember Doris always said that, no matter what happened, you couldn't start scratching your ear or rubbing your leg or, even worse if there was a fly buzzing about as happened on one or two occasions, you couldn't start swatting it. You might watch it out of the corner of your eye but if it landed on your head you would have to sit there until it went.

'Doris was very professional. It was very hot up there under the lights and she sometimes found it unbearable, but she sat there and sweated it out. She was a professional from top to toe. She didn't put on airs and graces. It came to her naturally.

'Doris always gave very good survival evidence. I remember one little thing in particular. I think we were at the Palladium, where Doris appeared several times, and she suddenly started talking about the old mountain goat. It sounded absolute rubbish. I couldn't believe it would make sense to anyone, but the woman she was talking to was astonished. It had real meaning for her. Apparently, the phrase was a family nickname. Well, it was so unusual you couldn't have dreamed that up if you tried.

'The great thing about Doris was the way in which she was able to help so many people who were really suffering. People whose children had been murdered or killed on a motorbike or died in a cot death or committed suicide . . . Doris had to reassure them and give them survival evidence, not just once, but in sitting after sitting after sitting.

'These days death is the unmentionable subject. You can talk about sex, you can talk about anything no matter how intimate, but you can't talk about death. People do literally cross the road sometimes to avoid a friend or neighbour whose husband has died.

'Doris would never do that. She had a natural compassion and warmth of spirit. She really could reach out and touch those who were ill or suffering or suicidal because she'd had a difficult life herself and she was able to appreciate the problems.

'No matter how well-known she became, she never lost the common touch. She was always thrilled to be invited to a posh dinner or a swanky night-out or to meet a star but she always said to me, "I'm still the same Doris Stokes," and she was.

'It sounds hackneyed but she became a celebrity that celebrities wanted to meet and it was a constant source of amazement to her. I remember once we went to a book launch at Hatchards, the famous bookstore in Piccadilly. She phoned up the next day and said, I met so-and-so and so-and-so and they wanted to meet *me*! She wasn't showing off; she was amazed to think that well-known people who were household names wanted to meet her. She could never quite get over the fact that the famous regarded her as famous and they wanted

147

to enjoy her friendship and patronage. I think it was endearing that the fame never went to her head.

'Doris could be difficult at times. She had a forceful personality and she liked to have things her own way. I never saw her bad-tempered but I did see her agitated before a show. Like a lot of well-known people in the public eye, she needed reassurance that the meeting would go all right.

'She really did give to an audience. Sometimes she would go on stage looking a million dollars. She would have her hair beautifully done, her nails beautifully done. She'd wear a bracelet, a couple of rings and an evening gown and she would look really good. Yet she'd come off that stage absolutely drained and it was all she could to to drag herself to the dressing-room for a cigarette and a cup of tea and a chat. She was damn glad to get home.

'I understand a little of what it was like because I felt it myself. I once chaired three meetings in a row for her at the Dominion Theatre, By the second night I felt ghastly and by the third night I felt actually ill. It was the sheer pull of emotion from the audience. It was like being a sponge on the stage and having all the water and energy wrung out of you.

'Now if *I* felt like that, imagine how Doris must have felt.

'She vowed after that she would never do three nights in a row again. Not only because she felt so ghastly and wretched, but because she felt she couldn't do her best for the audience.

'She was genuinely worried about giving good value.
' "They've paid to come and they've paid to see me," she used to say, "I've got to do my best."

'Yet as Doris was the first to admit, some nights were less good than others. She always knew when it hadn't gone so well and she never tossed it aside.

' "That wasn't very good tonight," she'd say, because she hadn't been feeling well or some minor mishap had occurred which prevented her from doing as well as she'd hoped.

'She could be her own worst enemy, too. Sometimes I'd think, "She's done really well tonight." There had been some excellent evidence but she would start apologizing over the few little mix-ups that had occurred along the way. She was never cocky about her powers as a medium.

'I used to get loads of letters from people waiting to have a sitting with Doris and obviously it wasn't fair to single out some and say, that I can arrange and that I can't. But now and again I'd get a letter or phone call that was so desperate I would break my rule. There would be someone who was on the verge of suicide or off work with a nervous breakdown because of bereavement.

'In those cases I'd phone Doris and, giving her no details, I'd ask if she'd mind talking to them. Never once did Doris say no. She would always phone that person and she must have spent literally thousands of pounds on her phone bills.

'As far as I'm concerned, Doris Stokes was honest. Sometimes the evidence was so obscure there was no way she could have known the details that she relayed.

'The point is, if Doris had cheated on a large scale it would have come to notice years ago. Some national paper would have paid a couple a few thousand pounds to expose Doris Stokes. Fleet Street had built Doris up, and when you've built somebody up there is only one thing you can do and that's knock them down. If there had been any watertight evidence against her, it would have been in the Sunday rags years ago.

'Doris made mistakes, and if she cheated she wouldn't have made mistakes. She was nervous before a big demonstration. If she'd memorized everything she wouldn't have been worried. What's more, Doris didn't have a good memory. She was awful at remembering people's names and, with the greatest respect, she was a simple woman. An ordinary housewife of limited education who didn't have the intelligence to make up elaborate stories or practise fraud on a large scale.

'In the end, it doesn't matter what the writers, researchers or journalists say, the thousands of people to whom Doris gave evidence will know she wasn't a fraud. If she saved one person from deep, black despair her life would have been worthwhile, but she didn't save one, she saved thousands . . .'

CHRIS HARE
Manager, Lewisham Theatre

One morning in the early eighties, manager Chris Hare drove to Lewisham Theatre, parked his car and then did a double-take as he glanced across at the red brick building.

It was still only 9.15 a.m. The box office didn't open till 10.00, yet a queue stretched right round the theatre and away down the road.

'We have a lot of well-known acts at Lewisham,' said Chris, 'Cleo Laine, Frankie Vallee, Victor Borge . . . and I wondered who it could be that was attracting such a response. I walked into the box office, very curious indeed, and was amazed to discover that the crowds

150

were for a complete unknown as far as I was concerned. An elderly lady called Doris Stokes. I'd never heard of her.'

Chris was even more intrigued when the information filtered through to him that the elderly lady didn't rehearse, in fact she didn't even have an act. She just walked out in front of an audience and hoped to entertain them for two and a half hours.

'I watched her first evening and I was amazed,' said Chris. 'I didn't know where she was getting her information from but it was pretty impressive.

'After that, Doris came back many times. Lewisham was her local theatre and she seemed to like coming. It was quite incredible. Doris was bigger than anyone else in the country – bar possibly people like Michael Jackson.

'We had to make special arrangements when Doris was on. We learned fast. At first we treated her appearances like any other . . . we accepted phone bookings and allowed people as many tickets as they wanted, but our phone lines were jammed for days, long after the seats were sold out, and ticket touts started hanging round outside reselling the tickets. In the end, we had to stop all phone bookings and we limited people to four or six tickets each of which had to be collected in person.

'As for advertising, I didn't need to bother. I only had to put a single line in the paper and we were snowed under. Doris wanted to know why I didn't put her photo in a nice advert like I did for other artists. I had to explain that I daren't.

' "If I did that, Doris, they'd be queuing over London Bridge!" I told her.

'The box office opened at ten in the morning and when there were Doris Stokes tickets on sale, people started queuing at ten the night before. In the winter it was very worrying. I was afraid we'd have someone die of exposure. I remember one freezing February when the forecast was very bad we had a load of soup packets standing by and we served soup to the crowds at 6 a.m. to help keep them warm.

'The funny thing was, they didn't complain. It became like a club. People got to know each other and I think they had as much fun in the queue as they did at the show. It was a real wartime spirit.

'I think about sixty per cent of the audience came because they believe in it and forty per cent came out of curiosity, but those forty per cent left saying, "How the hell did she know that?"

'At the theatre we all respected her enormously. Quite a few people were sceptical at first but in the end they couldn't find anything amiss and agreed that she had a remarkable talent. There was nothing fake about it.

'I remember a few little things she said to me. We've got two star-dressing-rooms at Lewisham, numbers one and two. I always put Doris in number one, but one night when I went to check it to see that everything was all right before Doris arrived, I noticed that there was a cracked window-pane. Now Doris hated draughts and I was afraid that there might be a draught from this window, so I moved everything into dressing-room number two.

'Shortly afterwards I went outside and bumped into Doris in the street. She was just getting out of the car. She hadn't been near the theatre, there was no way she could have known, but she looked straight at me and said: "You've moved my room!"

'On another occasion, I sorted out the money earlier than usual. With Doris, unlike other artists, you always knew how much the takings would come to because all the seats were always sold out. I got into the habit of settling up afterwards with Laurie.

'On this one night, however, for some reason I'd got the cheque organized early and I put it in my pocket, something I'd never done before, and went into the dressing-room to see them.

'Doris was sitting there having a cup of tea as usual. With some artists you have to lay on whisky; with Doris it was always gallons of tea. Anyway, she looked up and smiled.

' "It's all right, Laurie," she said jokingly, "he's got the cheque in his pocket!"

'I don't know how she knew.

'Doris' evenings tended to vary. There were times when she was in a bit of a state. She wasn't feeling too well or she was upset about something and on those occasions it wouldn't go so well. But then on other nights she'd arrive full of beans and it would go down a storm. Her gift seemed to depend on how she was feeling.

'There was one memorable night when comedian Freddie Starr came down and he stood in the wings trying to catch her eye and make her laugh. He would send her up outrageously and she could see him out of the corner of her eye. She managed to keep a straight face though, and at the end Freddie came out on stage and sang a song to her. The audience went crazy.

'There were a couple of times when we had to cancel shows because Doris was ill, but surprisingly no one ever complained. Normally in a situation like that, people are annoyed at the inconvenience but Doris' audience thought first of Doris and they were simply sorry she was ill and wanted to know how she was.

153

'I can truthfully say that she was the only artist who ever gave something back. She never demanded anything and she was always grateful for what you did for her. She even invited my wife and me to the *Psychic News* dinner dance and to her book launch on the Orient Express. I can't think of any other artist who would have done that.

'She also had a great sense of humour. I remember once we had *The Rocky Horror Show* on the week before Doris and there was a big poster at the front of the theatre: "The Rocky Horror Show" and underneath it, "Doris Stokes".

'When Doris arrived she looked from the poster to me.

' "I hope there's no connection!" she said.

'I can't say that as a result of meeting Doris I'm an absolute believer, but there is no doubt she had something I just can't explain.'

CHRIS MOTT
Previously Manager of the Odeon, Birmingham, now in charge of Odeon cinemas for the South West and South of England.

Like his counterpart, Chris Hare in Lewisham, Chris Mott had never heard of Doris Stokes and was quite unprepared for the Stokes phenomenon when it hit Birmingham.

'We were primarily a pop-concert venue and had people like Motorhead on,' said Chris,' and I thought, who the dickens is Doris Stokes? When we found out it was an old lady who sat in a chair and talked, we wondered who on earth would come. It was bound to be a disaster. After all the theatre held 2,500 people.

'Yet every time she came she sold out and there were still people asking for tickets. I'd have to go back and ask her if she could do another night and another night. Doris usually agreed although she often liked a free night in between to recover from the ordeal.

'I was never able to watch a whole show because I was working but I saw bits and my opinion wavered from scepticism to amazement.

'She'd give out a whole lot of names and you'd think, well, yes, anyone could do that. Then, suddenly, she'd come out with something so unusual and with such conviction – and it was always right.

'I remember once she told a woman that there was a lilac tree in her garden and she was to stand by it in the summer when it was in full bloom and her husband would be with her. The message meant a great deal to that woman. Apparently she did have a lilac tree in her garden (she might have lived in a high-rise flat for all Doris knew) and it was one of her husband's favourites. He loved that tree. It seemed entirely likely to her that her husband would be there if he could when the lilac was in blossom.

'There's no doubt that Doris gave people a lot of comfort. There were people who came back time and time again to her shows, but there was also a high proportion of new people.

'There was sometimes opposition to what she did. We had Christian fundamentalists outside the cinema handing out leaflets some nights, but it didn't stop people coming in and it didn't put Doris off. She'd often hold up a leaflet to the audience and say, "Look what I've got! Did you get one of these?" and she'd use the incident to start her talk.

'Celebrities often popped in when Doris was around. There were one or two knees-ups in the dressing-room

155

when Rusty Lee came to visit, and on one occasion Danny La Rue called in. Doris had been hoping he'd be able to come, but he was working, too, and wasn't sure he could get to the Odeon in time.

'Anyway 10.30 came and Doris was spinning it out as much as she could. I'd got the stage door open all ready for him and we waited and waited but he didn't show.

'Then suddenly the doors at the back of the auditorium burst open and Danny La Rue came charging down the aisle. He'd come in the front of the theatre instead of going to the stage door. He bounded up on stage and the two of them sang "On Mother Kelly's Doorstep". It brought the house down.

'I must say that Doris was always genuinely sweet and nice and she was the only artist I've ever known who rang me after the show to say, "How are you?"

'I mean, I've become friends with various artists over the years but the friendship hasn't extended outside the theatre. With Doris it was different. She invited me to her book-launches and various functions that she thought I'd enjoy.

'She was totally sincere.'

JENNE CASAROTTO
Director of Douglas Rae Management and literary agent to Doris.

It wasn't so much what Doris said that impressed Jenne Casarotto as what she didn't say.

Jenne had gone along to a small hall in London to watch Doris give a demonstration of clairaudience.

'She started getting all this stuff for a woman in the audience,' said Jenne. ''I've got Fred here,'' she said, and she was coming out with a lot of comments when suddenly she stopped, as if she was listening to something, and then said quickly, "Ah yes. Well, I think we'll move on now," and she abruptly turned to someone else.

'I didn't think anything of it at the time but afterwards when the demonstration was over I was talking to Doris when this woman came up.

' "I just wanted to thank you for stopping when you did," she said.

' "Well, it seemed wiser not to go on," said Doris.

'It turned out that the woman was with somebody she shouldn't have been with and "Fred" had told Doris. It would have been highly embarrassing to her if Doris had blurted out Fred's remarks.

'That impressed me terribly.'

Jenne had never represented a medium before and she heard of Doris quite by chance.

'Garth Pearce had written his first novel and I was acting as his literary agent,' said Jenne. 'He told me about this extraordinary lady who was huge in Australia yet lived in a council flat in London.

'Apparently she'd told him all kinds of details about his family. A lot of the stuff was quite unknown to Garth but afterwards his mother confirmed that it was true.

'Garth was impressed, and I was impressed that a tough, hard-bitten journalist like Garth should believe it. If Garth took her seriously then there must be something in it.

'Doris had written her autobiography and Garth, who'd seen it, thought it was good and that I should read it.

'Well, the book worked, and then I saw a video of Doris on the *Don Lane Show*, an Australian TV show rather like *Wogan*. Doris was a natural. She chatted easily to this guy, she was very good on camera and she came across as everyone's idea of the ideal granny.

'I couldn't have dealt with someone who drifted about in a puff of white smoke but Doris was down to earth and when I met her I realized she had a wonderful sense of humour which I liked very much.

'Basically, from a commercial point of view I could see that she had a lot of potential. It helps when you're trying to sell a book if the author can cope with the press and comes over well on TV.'

Jenne agreed to handle Doris' book, *Voices in My Ear*. She also began to see a lot more of Doris.

'Doris offered to give me a sitting but I said no,' said Jenne. 'I rather regret that now but at the time I was dealing with the business side and I didn't want to get emotionally involved.

'Over the years I saw more and more of her public demonstrations and I grew more and more impressed.

'I remember one night at the Dominion Theatre, Doris started talking to a woman in a box. She started going on and on about this woman's cooker. At last she went off the subject, only to come back to it moments later.

' "The man's been to fix your cooker today, hasn't he? And it's still not working!"

' "No, it's not," said the woman.

'Everyone laughed and Doris moved on. Then a few minutes later she came to a man on the other side of the theatre. She gave him a few bits and pieces and then suddenly she said: "Oh, my God, you mend cookers, don't you? Are you the man that fixed that woman's cooker today?"

'It turned out he was.

'It was a very funny moment and quite extraordinary. I mean it wasn't as if it was a local theatre where you'd expect the audience to have come from one small area. People had come to the Dominion from all over the country.

'Doris would never hurt people that was the other marvellous thing about her. If something came through that they shouldn't hear she didn't tell them. She was always very friendly and there was no weirdness about her.

'She certainly wasn't in it for the money. I never thought she charged enough. I mean she'd packed out the Sydney Opera House yet she still only charged £8 a sitting when she could have asked far more than that and later she gave up charging altogether.

'How she had the energy to do what she did, I don't know, particularly after so much ill-health. I mean, other people do interviews and they just talk. Doris always had to work to show what she could do, and I do think it was hard work.

'So many people tried to get in touch with Doris that we even got calls for her at this office. The tragic stories I heard. Well, I don't know how you even begin to deal with them. It certainly made me think about my own life more clearly.

'The sort of misery some people were in – well, if they could get any help from Doris – why not?'

ANDRE PTASZYNSKI
Stage Producer

The most remarkable example of Doris Stokes' powers that stage producer Andre Ptaszynski saw in almost a year of producing her demonstrations in assorted venues all over the country, occurred in Sheffield Civic Hall.

159

'It was a big hall,' said Andre. 'It held 2,500 people and it was packed. Even with the lights full on and the keen eyesight of a fifteen-year-old you wouldn't have been able to pick out particular individuals further back than the first few rows.

'Anyway, Doris was doing her demonstration and after a while she picked out a woman sitting right at the back. In a seat something like W26. Then she went to another woman sitting in the next row, picked her out too and said that they were sisters and gave both their names.

'This turned out to be right. Apparently, although the sisters had arrived together the place was so full they couldn't get seats together so they'd had to split up.

'Their mother had recently died and Doris was telling them about that and various names when she suddenly burst out laughing.

' "I'm sorry," she said, and her finger went right round the auditorium until it came to rest on a man sitting miles away on the other side.

' "I couldn't help laughing," she went on, "it's what they're saying. You're their brother, aren't you? You're a policeman and they're telling me you were absolutely furious at having to drive your sisters here tonight. You didn't want to come but your sisters couldn't get here any other way. Isn't that right?"

'It turned out that it was and the brother had also had to take one of the few spare seats left which was why he was sitting so far away from his sisters.

' "They're telling me that you would not believe a word of this," said Doris "and the only way to get you to believe it was to point you out!"

'Everybody laughed and although the man was embarrassed he must have been impressed. It was a remarkable achievement to be able to pick out three people who were together, yet seated separately, in such a large crowd.'

Andre first came upon Doris when she was virtually unknown in Britain.

'I'd heard about her from some friends in Australia,' he said. 'Over here, very few people knew the name Doris Stokes, but in Australia they told me she was a big success.'

Andre was always interested to hear of people with potential, so he set about discovering more about this Doris Stokes.

'I bought a copy of her book and I watched a video of some of her appearances in Australia,' he said. 'It seemed to me that she might do well here, so I tracked down her agent and suggested that I try her out at the Edinburgh Festival.

'Doris was keen to try so we got it organized. It wasn't a sell-out on this occasion. It was about half-full I suppose, and it wasn't the usual Edinburgh crowd. Doris' audience was mainly middle-aged women. Nevertheless it went quite well and there seemed to be something there we could build on.

'It took some time to build. First of all we put Doris on in a couple of theatres and advertised nationally. But it didn't seem to work. We couldn't get the audiences.

'Then, I don't know why, but we decided to try a change of tack. We went to Camden Town Hall and instead of advertising nationally we put adverts in the local papers.

'We couldn't believe the difference. About an hour before the show we drove up with Doris and there was a queue of about a thousand people right down the road waiting for returns.

161

'We'd certainly hit on the right way of promoting Doris. From then on she started attracting more and more attention.

'We must have put her on thirty-six times in all.'

Like many of the people Doris was involved with on a professional level, Andre never asked for a sitting.

'No, it didn't seem right,' he said. 'She did say once or twice that she could hear Polish voices around me, but then with my surname you don't need to be psychic to work that out.

'Yet she came through with some amazing things for others and she helped so many people. She was a wonderful woman.

'There was certainly something extraordinary going on there. Whether it was an example of something psychic or life after death, I don't know, but there was something I can't explain.'

The Charity Work

JIM AND JO MCDONALD
The Cot Death Research Appeal

The medium looked out across the audience and went straight for Jo McDonald.

'I've got a lady here who died in a hospital bed,' she said. 'She had been very ill. I'm getting the name Doris and striking blue eyes. Steel-blue eyes.'

'It was the blue eyes that did it,' said Jo. 'She had to be talking about Doris Stokes.'

The medium went on to tell Jo that Doris was passing on peace because she felt that Jo needed it. Everything was going to be fine she assured Jo, there was no need to worry and Doris was helping in their work.

'It was amazing,' said Jo. 'This was Sunday at our spiritualist church and it was the end of a terrible week. We'd had a few little problems with the charity we run and also problems at home. I certainly needed peace.

'It was strange because the message came through two years to the day since we last met Doris. The other odd thing was that after Doris passed I'd planted one of her favourite blue roses in the garden in her memory (she had a blue rose in her own garden which she was very fond of). Anyway, I always referred to this rose as Doris. That morning I noticed that it was in bloom with its first rose of the season.

'That medium didn't known Jim and I from Adam, so I'm convinced it was Doris Stokes coming back to encourage us on a very appropriate day.'

163

Jim and Jo McDonald run the Cot Death Research Appeal, a registered charity which offers support and counselling for parents who've lost children through cot death. They also raise money for research into this mysterious syndrome which is now killing more babies than ever.

'Every day in Britain five babies die of cot death,' said Jo. 'We had a near miss in our family – fortunately the baby was revived in time, but I'm also a nurse and I'd seen the suffering that cot deaths cause the parents.

'Usually there is no sign of any ill-health in the baby, there is no warning of approaching death. The baby goes to sleep and at some point stops breathing. We've had cases where it's happened while the child is being held in its mother's arms. Others while grandparents are babysitting and still more while the child is out in its carrycot or in the car.

'It's the most terrible shock and because there is no obvious cause the parents end up blaming themselves. They feel sure they must have done something wrong. Jim and I felt we wanted to help in some way.'

They set up the Cot Death Research Appeal and in 1983 they were looking for a president for the charity. Suddenly it occurred to them to ask Doris Stokes.

'We knew she was very much in demand,' said Jo, 'but we felt she was the perfect person. Her love of children was well known and she also understood the pain of losing a child. She lost four babies (three through miscarriage) and she had suffered the heartache and loneliness that comes when a tiny life is taken away. Who better than Doris to be President?

The McDonalds wrote to Doris introducing themselves, outlining the aims of the charity and putting forward their proposals.

'We thought it might take some time to receive a reply,' said Jo, 'but Doris phoned us straight away to say that she was honoured to be asked to be President and would do anything she could to help.

'We expected that her time would be limited but, as we soon discovered, Doris always had time to help people. We used to ring her and ask her to speak to bereaved parents and she never said no. She phoned them to offer comfort and was still doing so right up until the time she went into hospital with her last illness.

'She must have comforted hundreds of parents. She also donated substantially towards some vital research equipment that was required.

'On one occasion we visited Doris at her home in South London. She'd only just been discharged from hospital but she made us so very welcome. It was a beautiful day and we spent it in the garden. We sat there eating sandwiches and drinking tea practically all day and we felt totally at ease in her company.

'I'd brought a photograph of a baby who had recently died of cot death and I showed it to Doris. She knew nothing about him or his family.

' "Ah. It's baby Daniel!" said Doris as I handed her the picture.

'There was no way she could have known the baby's name but she was absolutely right. She went on to tell me other things about Daniel's family which were very accurate.

'Doris also made some predictions about the charity, which was very small and local at the time. She said it would grow and grow, spreading throughout the country and even overseas. It seemed very unlikely then but gradually things have snowballed and everything has happened just as Doris said.

'Quite honestly, if there were more people like Doris around, the world would be a better place. She was pure love. She found it very difficult to say no to anyone and she helped so many grieving people.

'She always did what she sincerely believed to be right and I don't think anyone could ask for more.

'I will always count Doris amongst my friends.'

WENDY SPRINGHAM

Close by two-year-old Amanda Springham's bed there stands a striking doll. Almost as tall as Amanda herself, the doll has brown curls, a pink dress, white ankle socks and shoes. She is also, at the moment, wearing one of Amanda's cast-off nappies. A bit of creative thinking on Amanda's part, this.

The doll, which is one of Amanda's favourite toys, rejoices in the unlikely name of Doris Dolly.

In an age when dolls tend to have faintly American-sounding names, such as Cindy and Kelly, the choice of Doris seems rather quaint. Yet there is a good reason for Amanda's decision. Her doll is named for Doris Stokes.

'We've never met Doris,' said Amanda's mother, Wendy Springham, 'but we feel close to her all the same. She opened a fête at Basildon Hospital in July 1986 and she bought a teddy bear and a doll to be given to the first boy and first girl born in the hospital after the fête.

'Apparently the teddy bear went very quickly but it looked as if the doll would never go. The fête was held on Saturday 5th and after that it was all boys until Amanda was born at 6.30 on the Monday evening.

'I didn't know anything about the doll, of course. I remember one midwife saying to me before the birth, "If this is a girl we've got a present for her from Doris Stokes."

' "That's nice," I said, "but I'm sure it's a boy."

'I was really convinced I was going to have a boy. I dearly wanted a girl but I wouldn't allow myself to hope for a girl in case I was disappointed.

'Anyway, at last at 6.30 on the 7th, Amanda was born. She was a beautiful baby: 7lb 10oz with big brown eyes so dark they were almost black, and just a little wisp of hair on top. It would have been nice if she'd had a little more hair but I was very glad she had those lovely brown eyes. My husband Alan's got beautiful brown eyes and I'd been hoping that the baby would take after him.

'As soon as Amanda was born there was a shout of "Get the doll!" I couldn't think what they were talking about but a nurse rushed off and came back with this great big doll wrapped in a plastic bag. Amanda's present from Doris Stokes.'

In fact this wasn't Wendy's first contact with Doris Stokes. Doris had become a friend of Basildon Hospital ever since the day she'd read a sad story in the paper about a young woman who had lost her baby because the hospital didn't have a foetal heart monitor. Had this girl been able to use such a machine, it seemed, the baby's distress would have been apparent and the hospital might have been able to save its life.

Doris, who never really got over losing four desperately-wanted babies herself, was very upset by this story and she decided there and then to buy a foetal heart monitor for the hospital.

'The first I knew of it,' said Wendy, 'was when I was taken into hospital early on Friday 4th. They weren't sure if I was in labour or not and they wanted to know how Amanda was doing.

'There had been some complications and they'd told me I'd probably have to have a Caesarean. Anyway they hooked me up to the foetal heart monitor and I noticed that there was a little metal strip on the top of it which said: "Donated by Doris Stokes."

'As it turned out I wasn't in labour, so they sent me home which meant I missed the fête. It was a great pity because I'd like to have met Doris. But the good thing was that when Amanda finally did arrive I didn't need a Caesarean after all. She was born quite naturally, even though they were all geared up for the operation.

'Amanda has been a real joy to us ever since. She is a lovely little girl. Strong willed but with a beautiful nature. She's always been very good and very loving. She's very free with her kisses and cuddles.

'I'm interested in what Doris had to say. My husband Alan is sceptical but I get very strong feelings. A lot of things happen that you just can't explain.

'When my mum and dad came to see me in hospital I showed them the doll and told them the story. "You've always been a bit weird," said Mum. "It doesn't surprise me in the least that you've got the doll. If anyone was going to get it, you would."

'Funnily enough, I've always felt there was someone looking after me and even in our house I feel there's something here that won't let us argue.

'There's nothing special about the house. It's just an ordinary terraced house, though it's quite large inside. We bought it from an old lady called Mrs Martin who let us have it for a very good price.

' "Be happy here," she said, "It's a happy house and I've been happy here."

'She was so nice, we became friends and I started writing to her but after a while there was no reply and I heard she'd died.

'Yet she's right about the house. It is happy and it's very difficult to have an argument here. Something always stops us and makes us think. I don't mean we argue a lot. Alan and I have a very good marriage and a good relationship. We've been together since I was fourteen – thirteen years ago. But now and again any married couple has a disagreement.

'Well, once we were arguing and a picture fell off the wall. Another time a photograph fell off the wardrobe.

'Something like that always seems to happen as if to say, "Don't argue. It's not worth arguing over."

'I'm sure it's Mrs Martin keeping the house a happy one. That might sound crazy to some people but I know Doris Stokes would have understood. I'd love to have had the opportunity to talk to her about it but of course it's too late now. It's a great shame I wasn't able to thank her in person for Amanda's lovely doll. Never mind, I wouldn't be a bit surprised if she was keeping an eye on Amanda from wherever she is.'

LINDEN LODGE

Doris always enjoyed any outing that involved meeting children and she had particularly fond memories of a visit she paid to Linden Lodge, a school for the blind in Wimbledon.

Some time before the visit Doris had attended a function at the Institute for the Blind in which authors whose books had been translated into braille were invited to a demonstration of a new aid for the visually handicapped – a moonwriter.

'A moonwriter is a machine a bit like a typewriter which writes "moon", a simplified version of braille,' said Margaret Grubb, head of Linden Lodge.

Doris was very impressed with the new machine and she decided that she would buy one to help blind children with their lessons.

She told her manager, Laurie O'Leary, the arrangements were made and not long afterwards they drove down to Wimbledon to present the moonwriter to the children at Linden Lodge.

'I hadn't long taken over as head,' said Margaret, 'and it was rather sprung on me. I felt a bit chaotic. What's more, I didn't know much about Doris Stokes but the staff had read all her books and they were excited. I think they enjoyed it most of all.

'She seemed a nice, genuine lady but quite disabled. She couldn't walk very far. It was quite a long trek from my office to the classroom and it was difficult for her.

'When we got there the children clapped merrily and Doris sat down to talk to them. She chatted very well to them asking them where they came from and that.

'She seemed to enjoy the atmosphere which I think is the selling-point of the school. It's very happy here, like a cross between *Fawlty Towers* and *Coronation Street*, I always say!

'After the presentation Doris couldn't cope with the long walk back to my office so she went straight to her car. But it had been a nice occasion and she clearly cared very much for kids with a handicap. It was obvious that she had a deep feeling that she wanted to help.'

The People

DANNY ANSELL

Doris couldn't help it, she was star-struck. She was as thrilled to meet a TV personality as any devoted fan. She never got used to the idea that she, too, was a celebrity and if a 'star' seemed to want to talk to her she'd tell all her friends about it for days. Just like any housewife who bumps into a famous face in the supermarket and exchanges a few words, she treasured every moment and relived the experience countless times to entertain her neighbours.

Naturally, she wanted to share her excitement, as she shared most other events of her life, with her readers and as her fame grew, so did the number of well-known names that appeared in her books.

She was often criticized for this. Some people accused her of only having time for the famous. Yet this simply wasn't true. Perhaps the books gave a distorted view because Doris always thought of herself as an ordinary member of the public. She had a tremendous rapport with the people and she always had time for them.

As she travelled round the country she gave comfort and snippets of information to countless thousands of people. So many that they became a blur in her memory and unless something really startling occurred she was unlikely to remember the details in order to record them in her books.

Danny Ansell is a typical example of these informal encounters.

171

Danny was a young surveyor working in the City of London and one lunchtime, passing a large bookshop, he noticed that Doris Stokes would be doing a book-signing session there that day.

'I'd already read one of Doris' books when I was about sixteen or seventeen and it had a tremendous impact on me,' he said. 'I just had this feeling that I wanted to go on reading it. I became very interested and I found it comforting in a funny sort of way. I rushed out and bought the second one, then all the others. I found them fascinating.

'So when I saw that Doris Stokes was going to be there in the shop, I bought four books and queued up for an hour to meet her.

'The first thing that struck me even before I got close to the table was that there was this very bright aura, if you like, around her. There was a tremendous feeling of warmth that was almost tangible. The whole atmosphere was charged with it, it was quite extraordinary.

'When I finally got to the table I'd just expected her to sign the books and that would be that, but it wasn't.

' "One of these books is for your nan, isn't it?" said Doris.

' "Yes, that's right," I told her.

' "And one's for your mum."

' "Yes, that's right."

'And she went through the four books and told me correctly for whom I'd bought each one.

'When she'd signed them she said, "Have you been promoted at work recently?"

' "No," I said. "Quite the opposite."

'I was quite upset because my position was about to come to an end and I would have to leave.

' "Strange," said Doris, "because I'm getting something about you doing better. I thought you must have been promoted but if not you're going to be doing something a lot better very soon.''

'This seemed very unlikely at the time but just after that I got in with a band (I'm a musician as well) and became a professional musician for two years. We managed to get a single out and travelled around Europe and had a thoroughly fantastic time. We never became famous but we had a very good time and it was a lot more fun than being a surveyor.

'Of course I had no idea that this was going to happen when I met Doris but I was impressed with her all the same.

'She struck me as a very kind person. She could have been anyone. She could have been the shopkeeper on the corner and she still would have been a nice person. The sort of person people would have come to, to share their problems.

'Anyway, after she'd finished talking to me I left the shop by the backstairs and as soon as I got to the floor below the atmosphere was different. All that warmth had gone.

'When I got outside I saw that the queue went out of the shop right down the street, round the corner and back again. I hadn't realized it was so long because I'd been near the front. I couldn't believe it. I'd seen that sort of thing at pop concerts but not for a book-signing. Some people must have waited hours and hours to see Doris.

'I walked back to the office but when I got there I felt very strange.

' "I'm going to go back," I thought. And I did. I actually turned round and went back, just so that I could listen to what Doris was saying.

'Once again the first thing that hit me when I walked on to the floor where Doris was, was that atmosphere.

173

The place was brighter and warmer than any other area of the building.

'It hadn't been my imagination.

'Of course, Doris didn't speak to me again because I was just hovering in the crowd but I listened to every word she said and I never forgot the experience.'

ANITA FLANAGAN

The phone almost slipped from Anita Flanagan's hand.

'I'm sorry,' she said, when she'd steadied her fingers round the receiver, 'Could you repeat that?'

'Course I could love,' said Doris Stokes. 'Ted says to tell Trish that he's met Joan.'

'I thought that's what you said,' said Anita.

She felt shell-shocked. Her husband, Edmund – Ted for short – had been killed in the Falklands war a few months before. Trish was her friend and Trish's mother, Joan, had died three weeks before Ted.

All this and Anita had not yet even told Doris her name.

'Some friends of mine had lost their son in the Falklands,' said Anita. 'They had been to see Doris and found it very comforting and I was in such a state after losing my husband they suggested I get in touch with Doris, too.

'We were so close, Ted and I. We had, in those short years together, what most people don't have in a lifetime. After I was widowed, I hated everyone. I just wanted to go to Ted.

'It sounds awful because I had children, but all I could think about was Ted. The children were upset, too, of course. Someone once asked my little one what she most wished for in all the world and she said, "My daddy home, safe and well."

'We'd always said that whoever went first would try to contact the other, so when these friends told me about Doris I decided to ring her.

'It was funny but once I got her on the phone I hardly said anything. I just told her I was a Falklands widow and I was desperate. She started saying something soothing and then she said, "Who's John? No, sorry, that's Joan," and the next thing I knew she came out with this message from Ted.

'She agreed to see me and we made an appointment, but when I rang off I realized I hadn't given her my phone number. I hadn't even told her my name. She still didn't know who I was.

'I felt absolutely shattered. I was supposed to be going out but I walked round in a daze, and then our puppy knocked over the bin in the kitchen. It was full and the bits went everywhere but by this time it was late and I would have missed my train so I had to leave the mess and run.

'The day I saw Doris my appointment was for 12.00 and I took my little girl with me. Doris was so sweet. She was like a granny really, full of love, and she was so good with my daughter. She obviously loved children.

'As soon as I walked in she looked at me and said; "He was in the navy, wasn't he? He was a petty officer."

'This was quite right. Ted was a chief petty officer on the *Atlantic Conveyor*.

'We went in and Doris started the sitting. All through she kept on about Ginger. I knew what she meant but I wasn't going to tell her. My husband's hair was bright ginger – well, flaming red really, but some people used to refer to it as ginger.

' "Who's Grant?" asked Doris at one point.

'Grant's my son.

' "Who's Cassandra?"

'Cassandra's my daughter. In fact, Doris went through and named all four of my children, and this wasn't easy because they all have unusual names. Apart from Grant and Cassandra there is Tarquin and Jocasta. Doris got the lot without any help from me.

'Then she went on and got my mother's parents as well.

' "He's talking about Alice Emma," she said.

' "My grandmother."

' "And I think that was William James."

' "My grandfather."

'There was absolutely no way she could have known that.

'She talked about someone called Angela who was so young to die.

' "Tell me about Angela," I said.

' "She was killed in a car crash," said Doris.

'This was right too.

' "Will you tell Robert to cheer up. He's not stopped grieving yet. Oh, and now Ted's talking about Australia. He says he's been to see Australia, 'and we could have made a go of it.' "

'This made sense to me. Edmund was due out of the navy in 1984 and we'd talked about emigrating to Australia.

'Doris described a big board on the wall in the dining-room on which I have about twenty photos of Ted in a big frame. She also talked about the mess I'd left in the kitchen the day the puppy knocked over the bin.

'And she said, "What does he mean by black and tan?"

' "Whiskey," I said. His favourite drink.

' "Now he's singing happy birthday to Irene," she said.

176

'This was quite likely. Irene is my mother's name and it was her birthday a few days after the sitting.

'After a while I asked if I could say something to Ted.

' "Course you can. Go on." said Doris.

'So I said: "I love you."

'There was a pause and Doris looked rather puzzled.

' "What does he say?" I asked.

' "He said, 'Naturally.' " said Doris, sounding bewildered.

' "Well, don't you love me?" I went on.

'Doris looked even more confused. There was another pause.

' "What did he say?"

'She hesitated.

' "I don't mind, tell me."

' "He said, 'Well, I *am* quite fond of you,' " she said.

'I was in tears by this time. That was what we always said to each other. It was always the same. It was a private joke. I said, I love you. Ted said, Naturally. So I said, Well don't you love me? And he would say, Well I am quite fond of you, and at that point I would hit him.

'It was a marvellous sitting and Doris gave me a lot of comfort. I needed to know that my husband was OK. I felt much better for seeing her.

'I became so interested that, some months later, I went to one of her shows. There was no message for me but it was a warm friendly evening and afterwards I went backstage to say hello to Doris.

'As I walked in the dressing-room she took one look at me and said, "Oh, my God, Ginger Flanagan! I've been getting that all evening but I said to myself, 'Don't be silly, she's in Portsmouth. She can't be here.' "

'I'd never got round to telling Doris where I lived and I think she assumed that because my husband was in the navy I must live in Portsmouth.

177

'We would have been married twenty-four years this year and we had such a fantastic thing going. I still feel close to him. I talk to him as I'm doing the housework or when the kids play up.

'I've seen him a couple of times, too. The first time was the first Christmas after he died. I was in the kitchen getting dinner ready and I was crying because he should have been there with us and he wasn't and never would be again.

'Suddenly I looked up and he was there. He walked across and put his arm round me. It was so real. He was warm and solid and I could even smell his aftershave.

'It's stupid really but all I could think was, "For goodness sake, don't you ever change out of those jeans?"

'He had this pair of jeans that he'd bought in America and they were his favourite. He never wanted to wear anything else and I had to sneak them out of the room at night to wash them.

'When I saw him at Christmas he was wearing those jeans and that was the first thing that struck me. Then within seconds he was gone.

'The second time I saw him was a couple of years after he died. My sister was visiting us and I was going through the jewellery box with her children showing them the different pieces. There were some of Ted's rings there, too.

'I took a few bits out of the box and something made me glance up and there he was. He was standing to my right, dressed in his uniform and cap.

'I just said, "Hello, love," and carried on.

'The kids said, "Hello, Uncle Edmund," and they carried on, too. It seemed so natural.

'Afterwards I took them all aside separately and asked them what they'd seen. They all said the same thing.

They'd seen Uncle Edmund in his uniform and cap, standing beside me.

'Children just seem to accept it. My little one was only two when he died and she could see him when no one else could and I often heard her talking to him.

'The strangest thing happened not long ago. I went on a trip to the Falklands with other people who'd lost loved ones there. After we'd been there a little while, another couple asked me to join them for a drink one evening. We were chatting and then they said, "Who's that man with you?"

'I thought they must have meant my son who was big for his age.

' "No," they said, "that big chap with the red hair we often see you with."

'I got out a photograph of Ted and passed it over to them.

' "Did he look like this?"

' "That's him," they said. "He's always with you."

' "Well, I think you've seen my husband," I told them. "And he was on the *Atlantic Conveyor*."

'They were pretty shocked, but it proved to me, yet again, that he's not far away and that what Doris said is right.'

MURIEL JOSLIN

It was her twentieth wedding anniversary the day Muriel Joslin's life fell to pieces.

As Muriel and her husband, David, celebrated their special day, their only daughter Sarah, a nurse, set off for work.

She never got there. On the way Sarah's car was in collision with a petrol tanker. The pretty nineteen-year-old, so full of life and fun, didn't stand a chance. Her car was crushed and Sarah died soon afterwards in hospital.

Muriel has three other children, all boys, whom she loves very much. She is also very much in love with her husband. Yet it made no difference. When Sarah died she just wanted to die with her.

There seemed to be no point in going on. There seemed to be nothing left in life worth living for. She seriously contemplated suicide. The fact that she is still here caring for her family is entirely due, she says, to Doris Stokes.

'I owe Doris everything,' she said, 'I wouldn't still be here if it wasn't for her. She helped me so much and she wouldn't take a penny for it. She wouldn't hear of me paying her.

'That's why I get so angry when I read the nasty things they say about her in the press. After she died, every time I picked up a paper there seemed to be something horrid written about her. It annoyed me so much, particularly as she can't answer back to defend herself.

'I've never written to a paper before but I sat down and wrote a letter of complaint to *Psychic News* I just had to put the record straight about what Doris had done for me.'

This is what Muriel wrote:

Dear Sir,

I am a regular reader of *Psychic News* and often read about Doris Stokes. When I lost my nineteen-year-old daughter three years ago, although I had a husband and three lovely sons I didn't feel life was worth living.

She wasn't only my daughter, she was my best friend.

Through *Psychic News* I went to three of Doris' meetings, and through her agent and his wife Iris, I was very lucky to meet her and her husband, John, at her home in London.

What a day. Doris said, come in, to David my husband. Go and make a cup of tea. David was unsure about the meeting, so Doris, Chris, my daughter's boyfriend and I went into the other room.

I was shocked beyond words at the things Doris told me. I had never opened my daughter's pay packet but Doris knew I had it with me and told me to the exact penny how much was in it. I opened it and she was dead on. Many things she told me about when Sarah was growing up that I'd forgotten but Sarah was telling Doris and although I was crying I knew Sarah was there with me. Many times when I have been very low I rang Doris. She must have had thousands of calls but she always had time for me.

I must stress there was no possible way Doris could have known anything about me before she met me. I also must stress that she did not want and flatly refused any payment.

I shall always be grateful to Doris for her kindness. Without this I don't know where I would be today. She was somebody very special whom I will never forget.

Yours very sincerely
Muriel Joslin
Dorchester

Muriel was naturally distraught after her daughter's tragic death and she went to several of Doris' public demonstrations in the hope of getting a message.

'I must have gone to about four meetings and I kept hoping for something,' she said. 'Actually I think there was a message for me at one of them but I was too shy to stand up.

'Doris had been talking to a woman at the microphone and getting a lot of things for her when she suddenly came out with all these details that meant nothing to her at all.

'She started talking about a man named Ernie who had a shop and was something to do with music and discos. Well, the man who ran the disco at Sarah's eighteenth birthday party was called Ernie and he did have a shop as well as his disco work.

'Doris also mentioned a big parcel. The person she was talking to was going on about a great big box. Well, at her party Sarah was given this great big present. it was huge. It was a joke from her friends. When she opened it there was layer after layer of paper and she kept on tearing it off until she got down to a banana and a bottle of bacardi.

'The woman at the front was quite blank about all this but it was so right to me. I wanted to say, "It may not mean anything to you but it does to me," but I just couldn't get to my feet and when no one seemed to know what she was talking about Doris went on to something else.

'Afterwards I was dreadfully upset to think that perhaps Sarah was trying to say something to me and I hadn't been able to answer. I was in quite a state and I went to talk to one of the women who was working there that night. She was very kind and gave me an address to write to, to ask for a private sitting.'

As it turned out, the address was manager Laurie O'Leary's office where thousands of similar pleas were handled by two devoted secretaries.

'First of all I got a letter to say that Doris was extremely busy at the moment and wouldn't be able to see me,' said Muriel. 'Then a little later I got another letter to say that they would be making an appointment for me.'

Muriel, her husband, David, and Sarah's boyfriend, Chris, made the long journey from Dorset to London.

'David wasn't sure about it at all,' said Muriel. 'He was sceptical and didn't really want to be there when Doris did the sitting.

'Doris understood this at once. She was so friendly she put us at our ease straight away.

' "Go in the kitchen, love, and make yourself a cup of tea," she said to him. I mean how many people would have said that to a perfect stranger?

'So David went off with John to the kitchen and Chris and I went with Doris into the other room.

'Doris was marvellous. She was able to tell me what happened to Sarah and she said that Sarah knew I was with her at the end.

'I was very pleased about this. When the policeman came to tell me, he said there was no point in me going to the hospital.

' "There's every point," I said, "I'm going." And I went and sat with Sarah. Of course, there was no way for me to know whether it helped at all so I was very glad to hear that Sarah knew I was there and appreciated it.

'Doris told me so many things.

' "Sarah's saying she was beside the railway line when it happened," said Doris.

' "No." I said, "That's not right."

' "Yes, it is," said Chris.

' "No, it isn't, she was on the road," I insisted.

' "Yes, but the road ran right beside the railway line," said Chris.

'It did, but I'd never noticed before.

'Doris gave a lot of family names.

'She said, "Who's Molly?" for instance.

'Molly's my mother and there were a lot of things like that, but she also came out with some very personal details that only very close family members could have known.

' "Well, that can't be right," she said at one point, "I can't understand it. I'm getting a girl's name but they're showing me a big, tall, dark man. That can't be right, love. Not Angie!"

'I was amazed. I've always called my son Andrew, 'Ange' or 'Angie', I don't know why. He doesn't mind and it's become a family nickname. Andrew's tall and dark.

' "Yes, Doris, that's my son," I explained.

'A bit later she came to something else.

' "Oh no, I can't say that, love," she said, "I don't like to say that."

' "Tell me what she's saying, Doris. Whatever it is, I don't mind," I said.

'Doris was very reluctant because she thought it sounded rude.

' "Well, she seems to be calling you Pig and Piglet," she said.

'I couldn't have asked for anything better than that. Sarah and I had pet names for each other. When she came home from work, Sarah would always call out, "Hello, Pig!" and I'd reply, "Hello, Piglet!" It might sound funny but it was an affectionate thing between us.

'Doris also reminded me of incidents from Sarah's childhood that I'd forgotten about.

184

' "She's talking about making lanterns out of swedes," said Doris.

'I couldn't think what she meant at first, then I remembered that on Guy Fawkes night, years ago, my father showed Sarah how to make lanterns by hollowing out swedes.

'She even knew that we put three red roses on the grave. Three was particularly significant. We always used to say that you only ever need three red roses – for I Love You.

'There was information for Chris, too. Doris said that she could see Sarah sitting beside him and she was telling him that she hoped he would get over his loss and marry a nice girl one day. She wanted them to name their daughter after her.

'I was very, very pleased.

'When she'd finished we all went back into the other room and had a cup of tea with David and John.

'That was when she mentioned the bit about the wage packet. The sitting was supposed to be over but Doris suddenly turned to me and said, "Sarah tells me you've got her last wage packet in your handbag."

' "Yes, I have," I said. "I've never opened it."

' "No, but Sarah knows how much is in it," said Doris, and she told me the figure.

'I had no idea whether it was right or not so I opened the wage packet and counted out the money. Doris was right down to the last penny.

'It shook David rigid, that did.

'There was no doubt that Doris was genuine and, as I said in my letter, she wouldn't take any money when we left. She wouldn't hear of it.

'I felt much better for seeing her. She helped me a great deal but over the next few months I still got bad days. I shall never get over losing my daughter. Doris helped me to cope but I don't think that the emptiness inside will ever go. I'm always wanting to tell Sarah some little thing and then I remember she's not there and I can't.

'Then there's the guilt. I feel guilty when I go out to buy something for myself because I ought to be buying it for my daughter. I even feel guilty when I laugh.

'Strangely enough, it's the younger generation who're more understanding. People my own age walk across the road when they see me rather than talk, but the youngsters come up and say, "Are you all right? Would you like a coffee?"

'They might wear strange clothes but you can't judge a person by their outward appearance. They've been wonderful. The young people, and Doris.

'Whenever I felt low, I rang Doris. I rang her quite often and she always had time for me. I never needed to say who I was, even the first time I rang.

' "No, don't tell me," she'd say, "I'll ask . . . Oh, it's Sarah's Mummy, isn't it?" And she always came up with some little thing to help.

'She knew that Sarah was buried next to my father. My father and mother had a joint plot in the cemetery but when she knew I wanted Sarah in with Dad, Mum gave up her plot for Sarah. Even so I used to worry terribly that they'd start digging next to her and put some stranger in. We've been able to buy the adjoining plot now, anyway, but it doesn't matter so much because Doris explained that it wasn't important. Sarah's not there; it's only her old clothes in the grave.

'She was such a lovely girl. She was my best friend as well as my daughter and she always wanted me along when she did things.

' "We're just going into town, Mum," she'd say. "Are you coming?"

' "You don't want me along," I'd protest.

186

' "Yes, we do," she'd say.

'That makes her sound like a mummy's girl but she wasn't. She was very popular and has so many friends. At the funeral the church was so full they were standing at the back and queuing down the street because so many people wanted to be there.

'As for the flowers, well there were so many we had to ask if people would like to make donations to an appeal fund instead. In a few months we raised £100,000 for charity. It was incredible. If it was me who'd died we'd have got £5 if we were lucky, but because it was Sarah we got thousands. People loved her so much.

'I still feel her very close. Sometimes we go down into the hall in the morning and we can smell her perfume in the places where she used to stand and do her hair.

' "Who's been downstairs?" people ask.

' "No one," I say, and they can't understand it because there's such a distinctive smell of Sarah's favourite perfume, Yves St. Laurent.

'She's particularly close when I'm in any trouble. Some time ago I had to have a very serious operation. I was rushed into hospital and I nearly died.

'I can remember going into this tunnel and I could see a light at the end of the tunnel and Sarah was coming towards me.

' "Go back, Mum," she said, "the boys still need you. It's not time yet."

'And then the tunnel went away.

'Afterwards, I asked the surgeon if I'd been close to death. He said I'd been very ill indeed.

'I'm sure that I almost went into the spirit world that day.

'There is no doubt that I wouldn't be here now if it wasn't for Doris. I was seriously thinking about suicide but she taught me that wasn't the right thing to do, and

187

if I did it I probably wouldn't be with Sarah anyway because I'd have to go to a different place.

'I sounds terrible to say, because I love my husband and sons so much, but at times I could only think of my Sarah.

'I've certainly got everything to thank Doris for.'

GRAHAM STEPHENS

Graham Stephens and his wife, Mary, were shattered when they saw the programme. They'd switched on because they'd read that Doris Stokes would be appearing and they were great fans.

They had read Doris' books and attended one of her shows, and though they'd never received a message they derived great comfort from her words. It was four years since they'd lost their beloved son Ian in a road accident, and though nothing would replace him in their lives, Doris' philosophy at least helped them to cope.

Now they wondered if they'd been clinging to an illusion. Instead of the interesting programme they'd been expecting, they witnessed critic after critic tearing into Doris. By the time the show ended Mary's faith was in tatters.

Could she have been wrong? Was the idea that Ian lived on somewhere just a fantasy?

In great distress she wrote a distraught letter to Doris.

'I read the letter when she'd written it and it was so agonized I wondered whether I should post it,' said Graham, 'but then I thought it wasn't fair not to. The programme had caused Mary to doubt, and she was frightened that she wouldn't see Ian again one day.

'I don't know what we expected. There was no guarantee we'd even get a reply but to our surprise Doris phoned as soon as she received the letter.

'She had flu at the time but she was so upset to think that the programme had had such an effect on Mary she felt she had to act at once.

'She explained a bit about the background to the show and then she said, "I think I've got your son here."

'And she went on to tell us so much about Ian and various members of the family that it completely restored our confidence. It really made a substantial difference to our lives.

'We'd deliberately told her nothing about Ian, yet she knew anyway.

' "Your son won't give me his name," she said. 'All he will say is that it's the same as his dad's."

'This was correct. Ian's second name is Graham.

' "He's got a young voice," Doris went on, "he only sounds about sixteen."

'In fact, Ian was twenty-eight but he had a tenor voice which made him sound very young and people often thought he was a lot younger than he really was.

'Doris then told us that he had taken some exams before he passed over and he knew that he'd got very high marks even though the results didn't come out until the week after he died. This was quite right.

'She mentioned Michael, Stephen, Terry, Eileen, Frances and Wyn – the last name being a surname. We could identify all these people.

' "He's got one gran over there with him but his mother's mother is still on the earth plane with you," said Doris. "Elizabeth."

'This was correct also.

' "He's saying, 'Give Elizabeth a big hug for me. She misses me and cries every day . . .' Now that was John."

'John's my father.
' "And Edward."
'One of his brothers.
' "Now he's talking about Andrew. He knows about Andrew."
'Andrew was his nephew, born a year after Ian died.
' "He says, 'Andrew looks very much like me. When Mary sees Andrew looking at her, I'm looking at her.' "
'It's true that Andrew looks very much like Ian.
'Doris even mentioned Chris, who is one of Andrew's older brothers.
'We hadn't given Doris any of these details in our letter. We attached great importance to saying as little as possible. Yet everything she told us was correct. It was a remarkable demonstration of her ability and it restored our faith.'

After the telephone conversation both Graham and Mary wrote to thank Doris. This is how Graham described their feelings:

Dear Doris,

When Mary showed me her (first) desperate letter I wondered about posting it, then I thought I'd better not interfere. You could see that she didn't know what had hit her – almost like another bereavement, as we have thought so highly of you since starting to read all your books almost two years ago.

We also came to see you at The Odeon, Birmingham in October 1985. You didn't have a message for us but we didn't mind as so many people were in much greater need and it was a joy to see you giving them such comfort.

As you evidently could tell, Ian is full of vitality. He got a Distinction in his Accounting exam although this was his most difficult subject. We are sure he is doing great things on the other side but we still miss his presence with us, as many people do – and as you must miss John Michael.

Please don't work too hard, Doris – especially when you are ill. It must be an awful dilemma when you are asked and can do so much, but in public you need to be absolutely on top of the work if you are to do yourself justice.

Again, thank you for phoning. It has been a privilege to talk with you and to know how you respond to an agonized cry such as Mary's. We won't tell you more about the family – then you can't be accused of feeding back information you have been given on the phone.

With our love and very best wishes,
Graham Stephens
Redditch

SHARON HOYE

Doris always received far more requests for help than she could possibly handle. She calculated once that if she worked eight hours a day for the next twenty-five years she still couldn't complete the backlog of sittings for which people begged.

It became impossible even for Doris to answer all her letters as she had done in the past. There were simply too many. Instead sackfuls of mail were delivered to her manager's office in the East End where two secretaries, Lesley Browcott and Sharon Hoye, struggled to cope.

Nevertheless, Doris continued with her private sittings. It would have been cruel to have to choose between tragedies. So instead Doris decided to let the spirit world decide who should have a sitting and who should not. Somehow, she believed, the cases her guide wanted to deal with would force themselves to her attention.

This happened in many ways. Sometimes, she insisted, a letter would seem to leap out of the bag into her hand. At other times a sufferer would arrive unannounced on her doorstep, appear at a theatre or get through on the phone.

Occasionally a plea would so move the sympathetic girls in the office that they would go direct to Doris to see if she felt the case should be moved to the top of the priority list.

Sharon recalled just such a case.

'It was the 18th July 1986 and I had a phone call from a man called Mr Randeree. He asked if there was any way that some friends of his could get in contact with Doris Stokes as a great tragedy had happened in their lives.

'He explained to me that his friends lived in South Africa, but would fly over at short notice if Doris agreed to see them. We talked for a while and I explained that Doris couldn't give as many private sittings as she would like to because her doctor had told her to rest, but when she was healthy she would give a public demonstration to help more people at one time.

'Mr Randeree asked me if he could give his friend Mrs Mohamed my name and office number so she could phone from South Africa and speak to me herself as I seemed understanding.

'Half an hour later, Mrs Mohamed rang. She had a very soft and genteel manner though from her voice I could tell she had been under great strain.

'I asked her if she had recently lost someone and through floods of tears she told me that she had lost all her babies. Her three daughters had been killed in a car accident. Mrs Mohamed, who was driving, and her husband had survived, though her husband was badly injured.

'Obviously they both felt very guilty. Why had they survived and not the children who had so much to live for? If only they hadn't taken them. She felt Doris would understand a parent's loss. To lose a child is a great trauma, she said, but to lose your whole family . . . She didn't know how to survive.

'I spent the rest of the conversation assuring her that her children would be taken care of in the spirit world and would be together. I tried to give her words of comfort but I knew the only person who would be able to help her would be Doris. I said I'd speak to Laurie and, in the meantime, if she wrote to Doris I would forward her letter personally.

'I told Laurie of the couple's loss and got quite upset in the process. Mrs Mohamed had said they would be quite prepared to come over to Britain at short notice.

'Laurie suggested that they came over for a demonstration Doris was giving at the SAGB the following month. They might benefit from the experience of a demonstration and he felt sure that when she heard about their loss Doris would agree to see them afterwards.

'I wrote to Mr Randeree, their friend in London, and explained all this. If he could let me know if Noorie and Adam were interested in attending I would make the arrangements as the tickets were no longer available.

'Mrs Mohamed rang back a day or two later. In the meantime, Laurie had spoken to Doris and Doris said she had to help them. I told Mrs Mohamed that Doris would love to meet them for a private sitting. She was so appreciative. I've never known someone in such distress to be so undemanding. She was very emotional and, feeling the tears come to my eyes, I passed the phone to Laurie who was very kind and chatty.

'Mr and Mrs Mohamed arrived within a week. The day of their sitting they came up to the office as Laurie was going to take them to Doris' house. I think it was an emotional day for all of us. They were such a lovely couple and after talking to Mrs Mohamed on the phone it was lovely to meet her.

'After the sitting they returned to the office. They seemed to shine a little as if a great weight had been lifted from their shoulders. It had been a good sitting, a little difficult for Doris to pronounce the Muslim names she'd been given from the spirit world, but she managed it.

'We all sat and chatted about the girls for a while. Mr and Mrs Mohamed had a little laugh and a cry, and after a time they left the office.

'Whilst they were still in Britain it was the Muslim New Year which was very upsetting for them, so Doris saw them again to help them through their grief.

'Being the kind people they are they later sent Doris, Laurie, Lesley and me a South African rug each, which had been hand made by their Zulu women, and they still keep in contact with the office.'

During the sitting Doris was able to describe in more detail what happened during the accident and where the family had been heading. She also named family members and local places. She brought out messages from the little girls and was able to describe their individual characters as well as their news of what was going on in the family home.

The Mohameds found it immensely comforting. Later Mrs Mohamed wrote to Doris:

My Dearest Doris,

First of all, Adam and I would like very much to thank you, John and Terry for having us at your home and the time you spent with us. We were extremely touched that you saw us and comforted us so much.

After reading your books I realized you are a famous person and we had our doubts that you may not see us but we were proved wrong and realized that there are people who still care . . .

We had a pleasant journey back but I cried so much at Heathrow Airport as I didn't want to come back home. It was very painful, Doris. Whilst in London I knew I was close to you and Ramanov. I'm all alone here again. I cannot explain what your books have done for me and I'm sure for thousands of people. May God bless you.

The tape you gave me is already in circulation and giving comfort to those who have lost loved ones.

Doris, I miss the kids so much it's beyond description. I have no energy to do anything. Everything is such an effort. My memory is no longer there. I have lost all confidence and thinking power as well. Everything is so dim to me . . .

If ever you have a message for us from our babies, please don't hesitate to call us collect. At the moment that is what we are working for and what is keeping us sane . . .

Doris, I don't want to be selfish but I sound like it. Here I am with all my problems, you may have yours and I burden you with mine. Please forgive me.

The only thing I want now is that our children should be happy wherever they are and have all the pets they wanted to . . . Please tell them to have all the pets they wanted to and do all the things they want to do, and do ask them to visit us more often, and sometimes I wish they'd make their presence known.

Once again, Doris, thank you. You do so much for everyone. I wish I could do something for you. Look after yourself.

Lots of love,
Noorie Mohamed
Durban
South Africa

ANNE WEST

Normally, Anne West is wary of strangers. Her life has not been an easy one and cruel events have led her to suspect the worst from human nature.

Years ago, when she was a different person, she might have responded spontaneously, openly, unhesitatingly to any approach – it's difficult to remember. But now she tends to hold back, to weigh people up and keep a little bit of herself aloof until she's sure.

Which is why her meeting with Doris Stokes made such an impact on her.

'I'm normally so wary of people I don't know,' said Anne, 'but the minute Doris opened the door I felt as if I'd known her for years. I was completely at ease and could relax as if I was in my own home. I thought she was wonderful.'

Anne West is the mother of Lesley Anne Downey one of the victims of the Moors murderers, Ian Brady and Myra Hindley, now serving life sentences for their crimes. Her pretty ten-year-old daughter was kidnapped by the evil couple, tortured, murdered and buried on the moors near Manchester. Brady and Hindley even recorded the child's suffering on tape as some sort of ghoulish souvenir to remind them of the killing.

That tape shocked and sickened the trial jury when it was played as evidence, and news of it horrified the whole country. Though the murders took place more than twenty years ago, that horror has never been forgotten and somehow Anne West has had to live with the memory ever since.

'I'd been wanting to see Doris for some time and I was so pleased when I got the chance,' said Anne. 'She didn't know I was Lesley's mother. All she'd been told was that a Mrs West who'd lost a child was coming. It was a shame because she told me afterwards that earlier that morning, before I arrived, she saw Lesley in the house. Lesley had said that her name was Lesley Downey and she'd come to see her mum. "No, lovey," Doris told her, "I'm afraid your mummy's not coming today. I'm seeing Mrs West." She didn't know that I'd remarried and changed my name.

'Doris was marvellous. She was a perfect lady and I believed everything she told me. She told me things that even my husband didn't know about. She mentioned streets that had been pulled down forty years ago.

'At one point she said she'd got a William there. Well, William's my dad.

' "Just to prove it's Lesley and William, tell me something that I couldn't possibly know," she asked. Then she said, "They're talking about Rutland Street." Well, Rutland Street is the street where I was born.

'She mentioned my dad's friends and a caravan holiday Lesley had enjoyed in Wales just a few months before she was killed.'

Doris named other family members who'd since died and even a policeman who had been involved in the murder case and had later passed away.

'It was funny because I'd arrived with my husband and a reporter,' said Anne, 'but just as we got there a washing-machine was delivered. It was very heavy so he went off to give them a hand with unloading it and setting it up in the kitchen.

'Anyway, a few minutes into the sitting, Doris said, "Who's Alan?"

' "Alan's my husband," I told her.

' "Oh, my God!" said Doris, "Your husband's here and I've sent him out unloading washing-machines!"

'Lesley told Doris that as far as she was concerned Alan was her daddy. This was quite true. She'd never really known her own father and she completely took to Alan. She really loved him and he loved her.'

This affection between them helped to explain a name that Anne couldn't place at the time.

'Doris mentioned the name Lillian, which meant nothing to me,' said Anne. 'We thought it must be a mistake, but afterwards I suddenly remembered the day Lesley had her waist-length hair cut. When she got home Alan told her she looked like a boy and that he was going to call her George. "If you're going to call me George," said Lesley, "I'm going to call you Lillian!" '

Doris always became very involved in the sittings she did and the case of Lesley Anne Downey disturbed her deeply. She tried to keep the atmosphere as light as possible but some of the details she picked up were highly upsetting particularly to someone as fond of children as she was.

She wrote about the experience at length in her fifth book *Whispering Voices*. It took her some time to get over it. The more she learned, the more she sympathized with Anne West.

'Doris was wonderful. I can't praise her enough,' said Anne. 'Neither can Alan. The day I got home after seeing her I sat down and said to Alan, "No one helped us when we lost Lesley but now I feel so good after seeing Doris that I want to help other people who're going through what we went through."

'We talked it over and we decided that we'd try to set up a support group to help the families of other murder victims. That was three years ago in February and now once a month we hold meetings for those people who live close enough to come. We have about eighteen regulars. The others who live too far away I visit and write to. We have people from all over the country, including Northern Ireland. Every story is different but the suffering's the same.

'It's getting so common now. Every day you open the paper you find someone's been murdered or a child abused. There's a lot of work for us to do – but it's all down to Doris.

'After my sitting with her, Doris put a picture of Lesley on her spirit-children board. Now I've got a picture of Doris in my bedroom and I always speak to her. Every night before I go to bed, I say, "Goodnight, Doris. Please look after my Lesley for me."

'I'm sure she is. And that helps.'

ANGELA RAY

Pensioner Angela Ray never met Doris Stokes but she feels a curious link with her.

'I sent Doris a poem last spring before she passed. I heard no more about it and I didn't give it another thought,' said Angela. 'Then in January I lost my husband.

'About a month later a clairvoyant friend phoned me. "Your husband, Alfred, came through to me just now," she said, "and he said to me, 'Look at page 140 of the book you've just bought.' I opened it up and there was a poem by you!"

'The book my friend had just bought was *Joyful Voices* by Doris Stokes. Neither Alfred nor my friend knew that I'd written the poem, 'The Land of Eternity', and I had no idea that Doris had published it.

'I was thrilled when I heard and also thrilled that I should find out in this way. It was much better than a letter from Doris herself. A real link with the spirit world.'

ALAN AND JOAN REYNOLDS

In March 1987, just ten days after the terrible Zeebrugge disaster in which the car-ferry the *Herald of Free Enterprise* turned over outside the Belgian harbour killing hundreds of those aboard, the family of one of the victims arrived to see Doris.

Alan and Joan Reynolds were still shocked and grief-striken at the loss of their only son, Jonathan, aged nineteen, his fiancé, Fiona, and Fiona's sister Heidi. They were desperately in need of comfort.

Doris at this time was very ill. Unknown to everyone she was already suffering the effects of the brain tumour that would kill her. It was only a few weeks later that she was admitted to hospital for the last time. Yet despite her pain she was determined to see the Reynolds.

Like everyone else in the country she had been horrified at the news of the disaster and she wanted to do what she could to help.

'As far as we were concerned it was the end of the world,' said Alan. 'Joan wanted to go and see Doris. I didn't know that it would do any good. I didn't think that there was anything after this life. Not that I thought about it much. I was too busy getting on in life but if I thought about it at all, I thought that when you're dead you're dead. That's it. Still Joan wanted to go, so I went along with it.

'I was very sceptical, as Doris soon picked up, but she completely changed our lives. The things she told us were so accurate you couldn't not believe.

'She told me things about my father and how he died of cancer that were quite incredible.

'She gave us a great many details about Jonathan and Fiona that were completely right – she wrote about them in her book, *Joyful Voices*, and towards the end of the sitting she even told us about our dog.

' "Penny's got a growth," she said, "Don't let her suffer, Dad. It's time she came over."

'Penny was our black labrador. Just a couple of months later she suddenly went poorly. We took her to the vet but there was nothing he could do. She had to be put down.

'As a result of our sitting we became very interested in spiritualism and started going to our spiritualist church. Since then, visiting mediums have given us quite a few messages from Jonathan and Fiona. One even told us they could see a big black labrador sitting between us so it seems that Penny's been back to see us too.

'From being a sceptic I've completely changed my ideas. It seems to me now that the ideas I had before were peculiar, not the ones I've acquired since.

'We have Doris to thank for everything. Without her we wouldn't have survived.'

JOAN REYNOLDS

'Doris was a lovely, lovely lady. If it wasn't for her I wouldn't be here now. I was ready to do away with myself. I just didn't know how I could carry on.

'She told us so many things that were absolutely right. She said she'd never heard such a lovely giggly pair as Johnathan and Fee. That was really important to us. It was such a comfort to know they were together. They were so much in love that it would have been dreadful for them to be parted.

'There were things Doris told us during the sitting that we didn't know about at the time but we found out afterwards were true.

'For instance, she said Jonathan was talking about a new suit he'd bought just before the accident. We weren't sure about that, but later we found the new suit in his suitcase in the boot of his car. Apparently he'd worn it down to Fiona's, the night before they left for Zeebrugge.

'Doris also knew about the closeness between Fiona and myself. She said Fiona loved us like her own parents, and it was certainly true that I regarded Fiona as another daughter.

'I remember once we were having coffee together and I said to her, "Look, pet, even if it doesn't work out with you and Jonathan (because they were very young and you never know) I want you to feel that you've always got a home here and you are always welcome. You know how much we love you. We love you for yourself, not just because you're Jonathan's girlfriend."

'And that was true. But as it happened things did work out between them and they got engaged. We were delighted.

'We all loved Doris. When she was ill in hospital we went to see her the week before she passed over. She was in a coma and on a life-support machine but the nurses said, it's all right, she can hear you, so I stroked her arm and talked to her. I like to think she knew we were there.

'Now I keep her photograph in the house and I give it a peck before I go to bed at night.

'It's strange to think that through this awful tragedy we've met so many lovely people and in a way our lives have been enriched because of it.

'It's still not easy. Even now I wake up some mornings and I think, how can I still be living without him? At times it's almost too much to bear and I wonder how people who don't believe in an after-life can cope.

'Sometimes, when I see these other young men and women going round, I can't help thinking, why mine? And it comes over you quite unexpectedly. I'm in Marks & Spencer doing the shopping and suddenly I have to rush out and blab all over the place.

'Without Doris' help I don't know what I would have done.'

Also present at the sitting was Jonathan's older sister, Sonya. Sonya feels very strongly that when such tragedies occur, people always forget the brothers and sisters who are left behind.

'Recently, after the Piper Alpha disaster, I picked up a newspaper and above a picture of grieving relatives was a headline which said, 'Lost: Fathers, Husbands, Sons . . . 'The list went on but nowhere did it mention brothers. The brothers and sisters who're also suffering seem to be left out in the cold. It's not that I want to be mentioned in the paper, just that people seem to think you haven't got any feelings. As if, if you've only lost a brother it doesn't matter. Whereas in fact my life has been devastated by the loss.

'That's why it meant so much to me to go along to see Doris with Mum and Dad.

'The first thing that struck me was how ordinary she was. I don't know what I expected but she was a perfectly ordinary lady in her dressing-gown, and obviously not-at-all well. Yet she had this incredible gift.

'We walked into her house that day and to say that the world was black for us was the biggest understatement of the year, but after talking to Doris we walked out again and there was hope. She gave us strength.

'There were several things that Doris told me person-ally that impressed me very much.

'The first was about my friend Trish. She said, "Who's Trish? You forgot to pick her up today didn't you?"

'I was amazed. This was a Wednesday and normally on a Wednesday I pick up Trish and her little girl and we go to a gym club for toddlers. Anyway, that morning I'd left in such a rush to get over to Mum and Dad's that I forgot all about Trish.

'I pulled up outside Mum and Dad's house and the first thing I saw was Jonathan's car sitting in their drive. I sat there looking at Jon's car and thinking about him, when suddenly it flashed into my mind, "Oh, no, I've forgotten to tell Trish I'm not going today."

'I went inside and tried to phone her from Mum and Dad's but there was no answer. She'd already gone.

'It was only a tiny little thing but I thought it was incredible that Doris should pick that up. A bit later she said that Jon was telling her how much he liked my new blue car.

'Well, only a week or two before Zeebrugge I'd bought a new car which was blue. Jon only saw it the once and we were rushing about, but he put his arm around me and said, "I've not had the chance to tell you I like your new car. Are you pleased with it?"

'And the other thing was about my blouse.

' "He's saying something about a pink blouse, Sonya," said Doris. "Is it spoiled or something?"

' "Yes," I said and that really made me draw breath.

'This was a pink blouse that I was particularly fond of. Only a few days before, I'd splashed bleach on it and it was ruined. Before Zeebrugge I would probably have cursed if I'd done something like that but now I just shrugged. I find I don't worry about trivialities any more. When a tragedy happens you soon realize what's important in life and what isn't.

'By the end of the sitting we felt much better. The little things Doris told me meant more than anything. She made a great difference to my life.

'I feel that Doris opened a door to knowledge and awareness and let the light come through.

'The world is a sadder place without her.'

All Futura Books are available at your bookshop or
newsagent, or can be ordered from the following address:
Futura Books, Cash Sales Department,
P.O. Box 11, Falmouth, Cornwall TR10 9EN.

Please send cheque or postal order (no currency), and
allow 60p for postage and packing for the first book
plus 25p for the second book and 15p for each additional
book ordered up to a maximum charge of £1.90 in U.K.

B.F.P.O. customers please allow 60p for
the first book, 25p for the second book plus 15p per
copy for the next 7 books, thereafter 9p per book

Overseas customers, including Eire, please allow £1.25
for postage and packing for the first book, 75p for the
second book and 28p for each subsequent title ordered.